THE TRUTH ABOUT
GREEN
BUSINESS

Gil Friend

with Nicholas Kordesch and Benjamin Privitt

HD
30
.255
.F75
2009

FT Press offers excellent discounts on this book when ordered in quantity for bulk purchases or special sales. For more information, please contact U.S. Corporate and Government Sales, 1-800-382-3419, corpsales@pearsontechgroup.com. For sales outside the U.S., please contact International Sales at international@pearsoned.com.

First Printing May 2009

ISBN-10: 0-7897-3940-2
ISBN-13: 978-0-7897-3940-7

Pearson Education LTD.
Pearson Education Australia PTY, Limited.
Pearson Education Singapore, Pte. Ltd.
Pearson Education North Asia, Ltd.
Pearson Education Canada, Ltd.
Pearson Educatión de Mexico, S.A. de C.V.
Pearson Education—Japan
Pearson Education Malaysia, Pte. Ltd.

Library of Congress Cataloging-in-Publication Data

Friend, Gil.

The truth about green business / Gil Friend ; with Nicholas Kordesch and Benjamin Privitt.

p. cm.

Includes bibliographical references.

ISBN 978-0-7897-3940-7

1. Business enterprises--Environmental aspects. 2. Management--Environmental aspects. 3. Green products. 4. Green marketing. I. Kordesch, Nicholas. II. Privitt, Benjamin. III. Title.

HD30.255.F75 2009

658.4'083--dc22

2009013940

Publisher
Paul Boger

Associate Publisher
Greg Wiegand

Acquisitions Editor
Rick Kughen

Development Editor
Rick Kughen

Technical Editor
Beatrice Aranow

Publicist
Lisa Jacobson-Brown

Executive Marketing Manager
Judi Morrison

Cover and Interior Designs
Stuart Jackman,
Dorling Kindersley

Managing Editor
Kristy Hart

Project Editor
Jovana San Nicolas-Shirley

Copy Editor
Apostrophe Editing Services

Design Manager
Sandra Schroeder

Senior Compositor
Gloria Schurick

Proofreader
Water Crest Publishing, Inc.

Manufacturing Buyer
Dan Uhrig

Reviewer
Beatrice Aranow

This book is dedicated to my father, Chaim H. Friend,
who set my mind in motion.
May his memory be for a blessing.

This book is printed on paper
made with
30% post-consumer
recycled fiber.

Part VII The Truth About Green Procurement

Part VIII The Truth About Green Buildings

Part IX The Truth About Green IT

Part X The Truth About Green Management

Part XI The Truth About Green Finance

Part XII The Truth About Green Futures

Note: Appendix B is available online at no charge at
www.informit.com/title/9780789739407.

APPENDIX B Resources

Introduction

About this book—Green business, increasingly, is big business. Whether driven by market expectations, climate change, shifting regulations, or simply a commitment to do the right thing, green business has moved rapidly from the periphery to the mainstream and holds promise for businesses of every size in every sector.

Green isn't just about environment. It also represents a way of seeing your business, and the challenges it faces, through a new lens—a lens that can bring both risks and opportunities into focus.

The promise plays out at the micro scale—the individual enterprise—in direct opportunities to put money in the pockets of owners, shareholders, and employees by cutting wasteful spending on excessive resource use.

And it plays out at the macro scale—national, regional, and municipal economies—with impacts on jobs, economic development, balance of payments, and quality of life. And—just maybe—it's the engine to power us out of our current financial crises by investing in a new energy economy and clean new infrastructure.

This is not a book about treehuggers' rhapsodic dreams (not that there's anything wrong with dreams) but about the hard-nosed realities of business—and about the innovative new course being set by some of the world's best companies, large and small.

It offers a distillation of my nearly 40 years of experience, in business, government, and the civic sector, bridging the commonly assumed but ultimately false conflicts between business and environment. And it builds on lessons learned over ten years as founder and CEO of Natural Logic, a strategy consultancy that has had the honor to work with clients as diverse as Hewlett-Packard and Odwalla, Conair and Levi Straus & Co., and the city of Berkeley and the World Bank to apply these ideas in the laboratory of the real world.

The Truth About Green Business is designed to help you tackle these grand ideas in simple, practical, profitable, bite-sized chunks. It's intentionally brief, focused, and straightforward, and not encyclopedic (though I refer you to some books that are encyclopedic in the "Resources" appendix available online at www.informit.com/title/9780789739407).

This book is organized into 12 sections (plus appendices available for free download at www.informit.com/title/9780789739407) that summarize the major themes you need to understand to get your business on this new road. These sections include 52 bite-sized Truths that give you practical steps to take and key questions to explore to put these ideas into practice. Profitably.

How to use this book— *The Truth About Green Business* is modular and flexible. Feel free to read it cover to cover or to skip around based on what interests you; you'll notice recurring themes and lots of inter-related material.

This book is not only short, it's also inevitably incomplete. Green business is a rapidly changing field, one in which the best technologies and techniques are evolving daily, so no book on the subject can stay completely up to date for long. It was up to date at the time I wrote it and won't be by the time you read it.

I've done three things to address that:

1. I back up the "how to" specifics with timeless grounding principles that can help you think wisely to apply these Truths in inevitably changing situations.

2. I provide a "Resources" appendix with references to key books that can take you deeper and links to some of the Web sites that I use to stay on top of this field. You can find it online at www.informit.com/title/9780789739407.

3. I invite you to visit me online at www.natlogic.com/truth and my blog http://blogs.natlogic.com/friend/ and Tweetstream www.twitter.com/gfriend. You can sign up for seminars and online webinars that take you deeper; participate in discussions with me, my team, and other readers dealing with challenges similar to yours; and find out how Natural Logic can support you—with advisory services, education, coaching, and tools—on your path to becoming a greener, more profitable, and more satisfying business.

TRUTH

1

What is a green business?

The climate's not the only thing getting hotter—so is green business. The terms green, sustainable, socially responsible, and triple bottom line suddenly appear everywhere, from business press to mainstream press, from supermarket shelves to job boards.

Green is all the rage. This was true even before Barack Obama became President of the United States. You see it in product advertising, in growing corporate concern for carbon footprinting, in GE's push for $25 billion in new revenues from its Ecomagination initiative,[1] and in Wal-Mart's sustainability marching orders to its more than 60,000 suppliers.[2]

The scale of activity is new, though the trend itself isn't. My company, Natural Logic, has been working on "greening" businesses and economies for 10 years. We help companies build profit, brand, and competitive advantage, while reducing "waste," environmental impact, and risk. Apart from Natural Logic, I've been working to green businesses and economies for nearly 40 years.

But what is green business? What makes a business green? There are lots of definitions out there, some more meaningful than others. Green could mean that a business:

- Reduces negative environmental impacts
- Complies with environmental regulations
- Has a slick green marketing campaign
- Publishes a Corporate Social Responsibility (CSR) report
- Has good environmental management systems
- Is ISO 14001 or otherwise "green" certified
- Can sustain its operations into the future indefinitely
- Enriches the world in which it operates

My short definition of a green business (see a more complete definition in Truth 4, "Why now?") is one that:

- Makes sense, in both the short term and the long term (see Truths 50–52, which discuss green futures)
- Makes sense, for itself, its owners and employees, and the living systems that support it

- Operates lean, clean, and green (see Truth 13, "Running lean and green")
- Uses "green" to build profit and competitive advantage, and to reduce risk (see Truth 45, "Profit, value, and risk")
- Prospers by embedding the laws of nature at the heart of enterprise

The business leaders of tomorrow—and today—are going for both: business success and social benefit—making dollars and making sense.

The days of thinking of "doing the right thing" as being separate from "it's only business" are drawing to a close. The business leaders of tomorrow—and today—are going for both: business success and social benefit—making dollars and making sense.

In the words of GE's CEO Jeff Immelt, "Green is green."[3]

What it's not—The trouble with "green" is that it implies just "environmental." But sustainability—living and doing business in ways that don't erode the potential for future generations—commonly refers to the *triple* bottom line (TBL) of economic, environmental, and social benefit. As you see in this book, social benefit isn't just about "do-good." It's also a path to creating significant, durable business value (see Truth 45). More importantly, the presumed conflict between "business" and "environment" is a false one.

Green is not a panacea. Going for the green— and even getting there—doesn't guarantee business success.

Green is not a panacea. Going for the green—and even getting there—doesn't guarantee business success. You still need great products and services, impeccable execution, and stellar customer communications—all the elements on which a great business depends.

"Green" doesn't replace any of those, but it can provide a powerful organizing principle for business in the 21st century (see Truth 52, "Future proofing").

TRUTH

2

Why green your business?

"Well," as Joel Makower, chairman of Greener World Media, is fond of saying, "all the cool kids are doing it." Just as the natural foods movement spawned multibillion dollar companies such as Whole Foods, and the back-to-the-land movement has given way to the clean tech juggernaut, green business has moved from the cultural margins to the mainstream. Green business is becoming big business. (And big business is trying desperately to become green.)

But green is not just trendy. There are compelling business reasons to green your business, and the underlying drivers run deep.

Growing markets—The green market is large and growing rapidly. The "lifestyles of health and sustainability" (LOHAS) consumer market was conservatively estimated at $209 billion in the United States in 2005 and growing. Green building is a $50 billion industry. Eco-tourism is estimated at $24.17 billion.[1] Clean tech has become a leading venture investment category (a record $8.4 billion in 2008 despite the credit crisis and broadening recession)[2] and is one of the few sectors still projecting investment growth, even in these tough economic times.

The factors driving this boom include the following:

- Demands for increased transparency (heightened by the regulatory failures in the run-up to the financial meltdown)
- The need to support a growing and developing population
- Rising public concern for the impacts of environmental degradation, society's toxic burden, and the loss of biodiversity
- The looming challenge of climate change

Meeting these challenges—and addressing these needs—presents business opportunities that you dare not miss.

Good business—Green business is also good business.

Green businesses can

- Build operating margins by fiercely eliminating waste—whether of energy, water, materials, or opportunity—which cuts environmental impact and keeps money in their pockets.
- Build revenue by recognizing, meeting, and anticipating customer expectations for better, safer, and more benign products and services.

- Reduce risk by eliminating hazards to workers, customers, and the living world before regulators catch up and require you to—and before competitors leapfrog you and eat your lunch.

Green business is also good business.

There are many other benefits, perhaps less obvious, but no less important, including the following:

- Driving innovation
- Regulatory insulation
- Access to markets and license to operate
- Employee recruitment, engagement, productivity, and retention

The world needs it—In a world of rising populations and rising expectations, where most major resource systems on which human economies depend are in decline, where national security depends as much on reliable and affordable energy and water resources as it does on armies, and where the impacts of climate change threaten to exceed even the pessimistic projections, learning how to do business and meet human needs without "eating the seed corn" (destroying the very resources needed to ensure a viable future) is just the right thing to do.

Some people consider "it's the right thing to do" to be a soft-headed way to run a business and favor a hard-nosed "it's only business" approach that doesn't let values and social concerns get in the way of making a buck. And most people that I've talked with—in business, in government, and in environmental organizations—have long assumed that "green" comes at the expense of profits, and that they had to choose one or the other.

The truth is that it's not an either/or choice. If "green" can be profitable—and I'll show you how it can be—and if your business can be more successful "doing the right thing," why in the world would you not go green? Because what can be more satisfying than going home at the end of the work day (or at the end of your career) and saying that you contributed to the quality of life in the world around you *and* put money in the pockets of your family, employees, and shareholders? Why choose between one or the other when you can have both?

7

...if your business can be more successful "doing the right thing," why in the world would you not go green?

Why it's important—Each reader will assign a different relative importance to each of the factors I discuss in this book. But I suspect that two or three of these issues probably have your attention already—and more will as the next year or two unfold.

I can't decide for you how important any of these should be for your business or whether "green" is something for your business to merely keep an eye on, to investigate more actively, or to organize itself around. But my guess—and the premise of this book—is that you and your customers, suppliers, and employees will be paying a great deal more attention to green in the years to come. This book is designed to be a practical guidebook to help you do that successfully.

TRUTH

3

How to approach greening your business

Lots of big green ideas are tossed around these days. Green is reinventing business. Green is creating a new industrial revolution. Green is building a new energy economy.

Behind the big picture and the grand ideas, however, green business is also about basic, pragmatic business and good common sense—but with some new distinctions to consider and a few new questions to ask.

How to approach the work— In my work with hundreds of companies—whether global manufacturers or local retailers— over the past few decades, I find that our clients inevitably face three major challenges: strategy, feedback, and implementation. I suspect your company is no different.

> ...behind the big picture and the grand ideas, green business is also about basic, pragmatic business and good common sense....

Strategy is the challenge of charting your course across an uncertain strategic landscape, identifying the risks and opportunities, seen and unseen, current and emerging, it presents to you. Next, you must honestly evaluate your organization's capacities to exploit them.

To do this—to cross foreign terrain with the confidence of a seasoned explorer, and to enable your team to adapt and thrive in the uncertain futures we all face—you need to

- Understand what business you're really in—your true value proposition.
- Embrace goals sufficient to both the challenges the global economy faces and the opportunities available to your organization.
- Constantly increase your expectations, and don't settle for "good enough."
- Fully evaluate and account for the costs and benefits you're likely missing, so you can capture the value you're likely leaving on the table right now.

Feedback is the challenge of reading the signs—gathering and delivering timely, relevant performance feedback that enables an organization to stay on course. Simply put: Knowing where you are and where you're heading gives you a far better chance of getting there. So it's essential to

- Measure what matters—from value drivers to greenhouse gases—and continually benchmark best practices, both against competitors and across your organization.
- Deploy interactive dashboards that track and drive performance.
- Choose financial tools that don't leave money on the table, and that your people can understand and use.
- Build reports that don't just report, but that also change thinking and that turn performance tracking into generative feedback that supports better decision making.

Implementation, of course, is the bottom line: the challenge of making it go. Good ideas and grand strategies are worth nothing if you can't embed them in your organization, implement them effectively, and consistently harvest the benefits. To do that successfully, you need to

- Pay attention to the right things. "The wastes you've been watching in the past," Chauncey Bell observes, "are not the wastes you will need to be watching in the future."
- Improve operations and productivity.
- Communicate, engage, and coordinate through powerful conversations.
- Engage the creativity of your entire value chain.
- Turn supply chain management into supply chain value creating partnerships.
- Streamline management systems.
- Get your entire team on the same page to reap the dual benefits of creativity and coherence.

Strategy. Feedback. Implementation. You must master all three if you want to be assured of powerful, profitable results.

Where to start—This work lives in the mind, hands, and heart. There are critical things you need to know:

This work lives in the mind, hands, and heart.

- What things really cost (see Truth 46, "Reality-based accounting").

- How to guide your actions by the laws of nature (see Truth 9, "Secrets hiding in plain sight").

- How to read, navigate, and stay ahead of market and regulatory trends (see Truth 32, "Clearing the rising bar," and Truths 50–52, which cover green futures).

There are essential things you need to do:

- Drop the assumption that you have to choose between making money and making sense.

- Eliminate "waste" of all kinds (see Truth 11, "Waste? Not! Eliminating non-product").

- Use resources that are renewable, cyclical, and edible (safely metabolizable by living things).

- Pay attention to the physical life (see Truth 42, "Keeping score") of your business and the physical life of the living systems that support it (see Truth 46).

- Be forward thinking and future-oriented.

- Start "where you are, with what you have"[1] and do what you can.

Drop the assumption that you have to choose between making money and making sense.

And there are fundamental realizations you need to face: what business you're really in and what you're really here to do—in your business, and in your life.

I'll explain and unpack all these and more in the truths that follow.

TRUTH

4

Why now?

"Why now?" should really be "why not yesterday?" There are a multitude of global trends signaling a need for sustainable business—climate change, population increase, rapidly developing nations, resource depletion, environmental degradation, society's toxic burden, the loss of biodiversity, the prospect of peak oil, and more. The bottom line is that we need to learn to do more with less—both less stuff and less impact on the environment.

These trends are moving faster than ever, driving an increasingly uncertain world for business. Being green is a way to find certainty in today's shifting world and to deal with market pressures driving businesses to be greener. (For example, Wal-Mart has declared that its suppliers must use sustainable packaging to keep access to the retail giant's shelves.) It's a whole new ball game.

If you don't lead the way on sustainability, you're likely to be left in the dust by your competitors. In fact, odds are that other companies around the world are already working on it. You can wait for certainty, or you can lead the way.

As information becomes more transparent to consumers, investors, and regulators, there are new expectations for businesses to be green—and to be able to prove it. Add to the mix a new administration in the United States that has declared its intentions to build a greener economy, and we've reached a sustainability tipping point.

Besides, every day your business continues to burn more energy than you truly need, to produce non-product that you can't sell, is another day of pouring money and resources down the drain.

What now?—A couple of years ago, a client asked me a provocative question: "If we really took this on—if we went beyond baby steps and really told ourselves the truth of what was required—what would we need to know and do?"

The following "Declaration of Leadership for Sustainable Business" was my response. It's intentionally both terse and provocative. Its purpose: to challenge already good companies, developers, designers, and public authorities to an even higher level of thinking, aspiration, and performance. I think it provides a useful "big picture" frame for the nuts and bolts that you'll find in the truths that follow.

Because:

- The well being of our economy fundamentally depends on the services from nature that support it.

- Business activity has a profound impact on the ability of nature to sustainably provide those services.

- We are committed, as business and community leaders, to the well being of both economic and ecological systems, of both humans and other living things.

- We believe that these goals are compatible (and where they seem to be incompatible, we are committed to finding better ways to do business that make them compatible).

...every day you continue to burn more energy than you truly need, to produce non-product that you can't sell, is another day of pouring money and resources down the drain.

We envision our company, suppliers and customers, and our community doing business in ways that:

- Preserve, protect, and ultimately enhance the living systems—of this region, and the planet—that sustain our business and the larger human economy.

- Provide ever greater value in meeting the real needs of our customers, suppliers, and communities.

- Meet human needs in the most efficient and economical means possible, in order to include the greatest percentage of humanity.

To do this, we will:

- Consider the requirements of the earth's living systems in all design and operating decisions.

- Not take more from the earth that it can sustainably provide.

- Not provide to the earth more than it can sustainably absorb.

- Analyze the life cycle operating costs and impacts of our facilities, operations, and products/services, as well as their initial costs.

- Work to eliminate "waste" of all kinds from our operations, and to find safe, productive uses for any "non-product" that we are not yet able to eliminate.

- Treat employees, customers, suppliers, and stakeholders fairly, honestly, and respectfully.
- Take responsibility for the safety of our products/services in their intended use.
- Take responsibility for the safety of our activities for employees and communities.
- Take responsibility for the safe "end of life" recovery and reuse or recycling of our products.
- Design our facilities, operations, and products/services to be ever more efficient, ever less dependent on materials and activities that poison, degrade or encroach on living systems, and ever more supportive of these approaches.
- Do all these in a way that supports our economic well-being, and the economic well-being of those who depend on us.

We will measure our progress by the trends of our:

- Resource productivity (unit of benefit provided per unit of resource used)
- "Non-product" output (amounts and toxicity of "unsalable" materials and chemicals, formerly called "waste")
- Net carbon emissions (production of climate-changing greenhouse gasses)
- Ecological footprint (demand on earth's regenerative capacity)
- Profit, both near- and long-term

We will pursue these steps with a commitment to:

- Future generations
- Continuous improvement
- Open dialogue with our customers, stockholders, suppliers, and communities

What you need to do—Keep reading! This is a big field, too big for one book to cover, so this is not the only book you need (see Appendix B, "Resources," online at www.informit.com/title/9780789739407 for some additional suggestions), but it's the only one you need to start.

So lets get started!

TRUTH

5

Climate change and your business

Climate change refers to any significant change in measures of climate (such as temperature, precipitation, or wind) lasting for an extended period (decades or longer).[1] Global warming is the climate change on everyone's mind—the possibility (or the overwhelming likelihood, depending on how you read the data) that we face significant planetary warming, sea level rise, and other disruptive changes, in this century.

Climate change can result from the following:

- Natural factors, such as changes in the sun's intensity or slow changes in the Earth's orbit around the sun
- Natural processes within the climate system (for example, changes in ocean circulation)
- Human activities that change the atmosphere's composition (for example, through burning fossil fuels) and the Earth's land surface (for example, deforestation, reforestation, urbanization, desertification, and so on)

In the last 200 years, humans have significantly changed the atmospheric concentration of greenhouse gases (including carbon dioxide, methane, nitrous oxide, tetrafluoromethane, hexafluoroethane, sulfur hexafluoride, and hydrofluorocarbons), which trap the sun's heat energy in the earth's atmosphere, resulting in global warming. We've done this largely by greatly increasing burning of fossil fuels—and building an economy dependent on fossil fuels—and by reducing the capacity of natural systems to take GHGs out of the atmosphere.

How can it affect your business?—Climate change is changing the way the world gets food, does business, and lives in general. Some regions see stronger effects than others, but the change is global. Because of its widespread effects—which we are already beginning to see—climate change affects business directly. Climate change poses new physical challenges to business operations; for example, scientists are forecasting the following:

- Unpredictable changes in the intensity of weather (that is, stronger storms)

- Rising sea level as arctic ice melts and ocean water thermally expands
- Shifts in the location and amount of precipitation
- Changes in ocean currents that could make regions much warmer—or colder—very quickly
- Nonlinear changes to the climate—that is, changes that could accelerate unexpectedly

These changes affect business directly—impacting locations, methods, and costs of operations from sourcing to shipping and sales—and indirectly—such as where the workforce lives as sea level rise renders coastal regions uninhabitable. Scientists fear that changes in global temperature could wreak havoc on ocean currents, which are a key factor in driving local climate; as a result, various regions could become much colder or warmer quickly. In worst-case (but not unlikely) scenarios, shortages and changes in resource availability could drive political instability.

The challenge posed by the world's scientists is stark: to reduce global GHGs 80 percent below 1990 levels by 2050.[2]

Society's ability to respond to climate change depends on business sector leadership in reducing greenhouse gas emissions, sequestering carbon, and preparing for events like increased storm magnitude. Improving energy efficiency in general, and reducing fossil fuel use in particular, are two key ways that business can fight climate change (see Truth 10, "Eco-efficiency: Good for business and the environment").

Unprecedented opportunities also arise for business. Companies that provide more climate-friendly alternatives—clean technologies, efficient practices, alternative fuels—all stand to profit as the economy shifts to decrease its impact on climate change. Additional opportunities might arise due to shifts in resource availability. As certain parts of the globe are subjected to the physical effects of climate change, new resources might become available. For example, Russia might gain access to oil resources and agricultural land that were previously buried in ice.[3]

What you need to know—Know that debate over anthropogenic (human-caused) climate change is over—or should be. The

International Panel on Climate Change is now reporting[4] with 90 percent certainty—an unusually high percentage for scientists—that anthropogenic emissions are driving climate change. Those claiming that climate change is a hoax or solely attributable to natural cycles are part of a small minority, often with economic incentives to cloud the message of the global scientific community.

Policy changes, from carbon trading schemes to carbon taxes, affect your business, by turning carbon emissions from a scientific issue to an economic issue. So keep an eye on both current regulations and upcoming legislation; local, state, federal, and global governing bodies are actively creating policies to reduce greenhouse gas emissions, and help society adapt to climate change and rising sea levels. Some important terms to know include carbon footprint, carbon trading, and carbon offsets (see Truth 14, "Carbon footprinting," and Truth 48, "Carbon trading and offsets").

What do you need to do—Carbon will have a price in the future, penalizing large emitters and rewarding those who reduce their emissions. Leading businesses are already taking action, and many are expecting their suppliers to do the same. Here are some steps you'd be well advised to take, sooner rather than later:

- Get ahead of the curve. You can view the upcoming shifts in the economy as an opportunity. Companies can be leaders by investing in the new low-carbon economy instead of reacting to the latest legislation. We already see new funding and new markets for cleaner technologies with lower carbon footprints.

- Determine your carbon footprint and understand your risk. Companies that measure their footprint know where they and their supply chain stand in the face of still emerging policy and regulatory responses. They're motivated by both reduced regulatory risk and upside business opportunity (see Truth 8, "Green regulations," for more on how to face regulation).

- Reduce your footprint. Find out where your biggest leverage is in reducing your carbon footprint and take measures to change it. Done right, this often results in cost savings due to optimized shipping and energy efficiency. Take these three key steps—in the right order (see Truth 10, Truth 15, "Reducing your carbon footprint," and Truth 48).

1. Radically improve your energy efficiency.

2. Shift from high-carbon to low-carbon (or zero-carbon) energy sources.

3. Trade and offset your remaining emissions. Don't make the mistake of buying offsets before profitably reducing the amount of offset you'll have to buy.

■ Avoid carbon myopia! Don't ignore other impacts on the environment while you focus on carbon. For example, the rush to grow crops for low-carbon biofuel could, if they're not grown sustainably, worsen soil erosion, biodiversity, and health of local economies.

The markets are coming! The markets are coming!—State and regional authorities have been in motion on carbon policies, not waiting for Washington. Landmark early policies include the following:

■ **California's Assembly Bill 32 (AB 32)**—The first statewide program in the country to mandate an economywide emissions cap that includes enforceable penalties.

■ **The Regional Greenhouse Gas Initiative (RGGI) of nine northeastern states**—A cap and trade system launched in 2008.

■ **The Western Climate Initiative**—Encompasses seven western states and four Canadian provinces. This cap and trade system, largely based on AB32, is designed to drive economywide efficiency measures.

And Washington is now on the move, with President Obama on record in support of "market caps on carbon" and the U.S. Environmental Protection Agency classifying CO_2 as a pollutant—which could then be regulated. The international community also is gearing up for the Climate Conference in Copenhagen in December 2009 to consider the next steps after the Kyoto Protocol. (The Kyoto Protocol is the governing international treaty to stabilize GHG concentrations in the atmosphere "at a level that would prevent dangerous anthropogenic interference with the climate system." Signed by 181 countries—but not the United States—it establishes legally binding commitments for the reduction of key greenhouse gases.)

But don't wait for the regulations to be sorted out. There are consequences to a "wait and see" attitude, especially when driving down your footprint and costs can make sense now.

TRUTH

6

Profit and purpose

Everybody knows that the purpose of business is profit. Right? Nope. "Everybody" is wrong. Not that there's anything wrong with profit. Businesses need profit to fuel growth and to pay for capital. (That's what return on investment is.) But is that the *purpose* of your business? Or is it a *cost* of doing business?

Look at it this way: You need to pay your utility company for electricity, but is paying your utility bill the purpose of your business? Obviously not—so why do we think that paying for capital is the purpose of business?[1]

What are you really here to do?—That's one key question I've learned to ask every client. What's your organization's purpose? What are your long-term commitments to your shareholders, employees, and community? What are the passions and concerns in your own heart that move you to do what you do? I've found that rarely is the answer just "to maximize profits."

Visionary business thinker Peter Drucker said, "The purpose of business is to create and keep a customer." To put it another way, the purpose of a business is to do what the business is there to do. Profit is the by-product of doing that well. It's a way of keeping score. And you don't have to sacrifice profits to serve your true purpose.

Whole Foods Markets CEO John Mackey says that businesses have a choice: "[In] the profit-centered business, customer happiness is merely a means to an end: maximizing profits. In the customer-centered business, customer happiness is an end in itself, and will be pursued with greater interest, passion, and empathy than the profit-centered business is capable of. Our most important stakeholder is not our stockholders, it is our customers. We're in business to serve the needs and desires of our core customer base."

Natural Logic's purpose: "To help companies and communities prosper—and to find and fulfill their purpose—by embedding the laws of nature at the heart of enterprise." (To learn more, see Truth 9, "Secrets hiding in plain sight," Truth 24, "Biomimicry—learning from life," and Truth 27, "Design with nature.") The purpose behind that purpose: To transform industrial society so that it works, in

...Profit is the by-product, not the purpose.

Buckminster Fuller's words, "for 100% of humanity in the shortest possible time through spontaneous cooperation without ecological damage or disadvantage to anyone."[1]

But it's not a matter of purpose versus profit. Purpose is profitable.

Businesses that recognize and honor their underlying purpose run differently. For instance, while U.S. automakers focused on maximizing shareholder value, Honda and Toyota operated with the purpose of building cars that delight the customer. Idealistic? Maybe. But which companies succeeded?

"It's not a fleeting fad," says Natural Logic senior associate Christine Arena, author of *The High Purpose Company*. "These companies are investing money in a way that creates social, environmental, and financial value. They can't afford to stop investing in this higher purpose."

What you need to do—How do you "invest in purpose"? And make it practical? And profitable?

- Keep your eye on the ball. Make your purpose visible and present in your everyday conversations. Serving your company's purpose should be a continuous, systematic practice, and all too often, companies visit the question of purpose only in retreats or mission statements.

- Put plans, alliances, and designs to the "Purpose Test." Does this option move you toward or away from your purpose? Identify activities that don't fit your purpose and drop or change them.

- But don't drop the profit test. You won't stay in business—no matter how noble your purpose—if you can't pay the bills. (Just remember that paying the bills isn't the purpose of your business.)

- Tell the truth—to your employees, stakeholders, and customers— and yourself. This means clearly communicating your purpose, truthfully measuring whether your actions and results support that purpose and bringing them into alignment when they don't.

- Don't compromise. There'll be plenty of people who'll tell you that purpose is pie in the sky and will cost you money. I don't believe them and neither do the best business leaders I know.

TRUTH

7

How green is good enough?

How high do you aim to "be green"? Match your competitors? Go beyond them? Aim for carbon neutral? Carbon negative? Zero waste? Which goal is the right goal? How good is good enough?

"Traditional" environmental management focused on reducing harm—gradually, in a public policy framework of advocacy and compromise—finding "acceptable" levels of damage that could be reached at an "affordable" price.

But for a truly sustainable business, "good enough" means operating in a way that helps both the economy and Earth's living systems continue functioning long into the future. The implications for your business strategy are profound.

Why it matters—Protecting the well-being of Earth's living systems is not only good for the Earth, it's also practical business strategy that drives innovation and captures value that's otherwise ignored. "Do less harm" simply isn't good enough—not when you could thrive by regenerating and enriching the living systems on which our economy depends.

"Good enough" means operating in a way that helps both the economy and Earth's living systems continue functioning long into the future.

Regulatory compliance isn't good enough either. Regulatory hurdles will continue to rise as development increases and nonrenewable resource supplies wane (see Truth 32, "Clearing the rising bar"). Customers are demanding more transparency and greener products while B2B relationships require increasingly better environmental performance.

Courageous companies set aggressive and public goals that demand both technical innovation and organizational breakthroughs. The goals are diverse, and often courageous. ST Microelectronics is racing to cut greenhouse gas emissions by a factor of ten by 2010. DuPont has targeted zero emissions, zero defects, and zero injuries. Nike aims to eliminate chlorine. Interface has a goal of "no smokestacks or sewer pipes." Wal-Mart is shooting for 100 percent renewable energy, zero waste, and selling only "sustainable" products (and admits that they're not sure how to get there!). If you aren't setting high enough goals, your competitors' innovations will set them higher for you.

> If you aren't setting high enough goals, your competitors' innovations will set them higher for you.

What you need (and don't need) to know—Know what you are "really here to do" (see Truth 6, "Profit and purpose") and what value you really provide to your customers. Do they want the product you sell, or do they want what that product enables them to do? How can that insight help you do more with less?

What you don't need to know: how to reach those stretch goals. Yet.

Lift your sights—How can you determine "how good is good enough" for your company?

- Council with your management team and stakeholder network (see Truth 41, "Engaging stakeholders"). Consider the purpose of your business. If you started it, what was your motivation? If you didn't, what drew you to this company rather than another? (I'll wager it wasn't just the money.) What goals would fulfill that purpose—really!—and just maybe catapult you to brand leadership?

- Lift your sights and set your goals based on the physical realities on which business depends. Don't let the status quo distract you. Use the Natural Step[1] to test your goals for sustainability (see Truth 50, "Certainty in the face of uncertainty").

- Invite compelling "aspirational" goals, to expand imaginations and give a flavor of who works here, what they think about, what moves them, without committing the company prematurely.

> Don't let the status quo distract you.

- Set Big, Hairy, Audacious Goals[2] (BHAGs)—Have a willingness to aim high and "bet the farm" if necessary.

- Remember that "Good enough never is good enough"—meaning your company needs to set high goals and then periodically ratchet the bar even higher.[3]

- Go public! Committing to goals within your company and externally can help you turn your intentions into action. Use Natural Logic's "Declaration of Leadership"[4] (see Truth 4, "Why now?") to:
    - Engage your company, suppliers, customers, and communities in ways that ultimately enhance living systems.
    - Provide ever greater value in meeting the real needs of customers, suppliers, and community.
    - Do business in a way that meets human needs in the most efficient and economical means possible.
    - Do business in a way that includes the greatest percentage of humanity.
    - Measure your progress toward your goals. What's your resource productivity? What is your ecological footprint? What's your profit—near and long term? (See Truth 42, "Keeping score.")

Ask the right questions—The real challenge isn't just to be less bad or to slow the rate of deterioration, but to actually build the regenerative capacity of the living systems that sustain the human experiment—and to make that a normal consequence of doing business.

How much "waste" do you think is acceptable? How much environmental damage? How much safety risk to your employees or community? This is a business book, so compare the answer in your gut with the answer on your balance sheet. Your job: Bring them into harmony.

Here's a clue: Ask the right questions. Not "Can we?" but "How can we?"

TRUTH

8

Green regulations

I often advise our clients to ignore regulations. Not to violate them, mind you—just not to let them drive the business.

Why? Running your business—not to mention your green strategies—with regulations being the driving factor is neither a creative nor inspiring goal. You don't wake up in the morning and say, "My goal today is to floss my teeth." You do it—it's a good idea to keep your teeth healthy and your workplace safe—but the goal that animates you is probably something more...animating!

Regulation is necessary, but it's often, as architect and designer Bill McDonough calls it, "a symptom of bad design." Unfortunately, there's plenty of bad design out there.

But while regulations that hold companies to high levels of environmental quality can be good for both society and the companies themselves, the fact remains that our regulatory systems are problematic and often resented. Regulations can be difficult to understand and onerous to comply with. Agencies might be unpredictable, or at best slow, in their response to business concerns, often without internal incentives for their own productivity or quality.

So what should you do about problematic regulations? Fight? Grumble and comply?

The alternative is what I call regulatory insulation, which is to deliver products and services so good and processes so efficient that you don't care what the regulators want because you're years ahead of their wildest dreams. Let your competitors spend money on lawyers and lobbyists, while you invest in design and marketing.

> Let your competitors spend money on lawyers and lobbyists, while you invest in design and marketing

The payoff is substantial and not just in reduced operating expenses and legal fees. There's even greater payoff in impact on market share and time to market.

Steer by natural logic, not regulatory thresholds—Comply with the regulations, but don't guide your goals and planning with them. Instead of reacting to regulations, start thinking about the driving forces behind those regulations. For example, some of our forward-thinking clients started phasing out bisphenol-A even though it was not banned yet—at the time I write this. They could read the writing on the wall: Because anything remotely toxic in children's products should and eventually will be banned, they're now incorporating these drivers in their product design process instead of scrambling to comply when each new ban is announced. By looking past the regulations to the clues in physical reality, they've eliminated a random factor in their product development cycle and can shift budgets from lawyers and lobbyists to engineers and marketers.

Don't wait for the regulations to tell you what you already know is true. Design what works before it's required. Create a manufacturing process that uses half the toxics and emits half the emissions as your competitors' process, and you'll not only pass regulation with flying colors, you can use your leadership to gain market share, license your process to competitors, and influence future regulations.

> The notion that better environmental performance reduces financial performance is all too often rooted in habit, not evidence.

Drop the assumptions and face the facts. The notion that better environmental performance reduces financial performance is all too often rooted in habit, not evidence. It's easy to make design improvements that cost more; it's more challenging—and more profitable—to integrate "green" into the design process by including stakeholder expectations and sustainability requirements into design specifications from the beginning.

Reengineer the regulations

- Regulations need good design, too. Push for regulatory reengineering, which means redesigning the regulations and regulatory process itself, with a commitment to the underlying needs of all the stakeholders.

- This is best done with an integrative process (see Truth 36, "Integrative design for green building") that engages all stakeholders and addresses their common needs: government needs enforceability and protection; business needs predictability and low bureaucracy; and nature needs both business and government to play by her rules (see Truth 27, "Design with nature").

- Map the regulatory system, as you would with a production process. Odds are there's lots of fat to trim—without lowering environmental protection standards—and trimmed fat means less cost to both business and government.

- Ensure that regulators know who their "customer" is, what their "product" is, and what performance goals are expected of them. Regulators are running a business too, and need effective management systems and staff training to build their effectiveness.

- Implement the redesign; measure the results and be prepared for surprises.

What's next?—Here are some things you can do to look ahead:

- Look at regulations from other parts of the world. Businesses benchmark their competitors; regulators can do that, too. In some cases—as with the European WEEE, RoHS, and REACH directives, and international response to the Kyoto Protocol on climate change[1]—you can get a heads-up about what might be coming soon to a regulatory jurisdiction near you.

- Use scenario planning (see Truth 51, "Scenario planning") to envision possible future regulatory systems and test your products and business plans.

- Lobby for "real-time regulation" to streamline monitoring and enforcement (see Truth 39, "How IT can drive greening").

TRUTH

9

Secrets hiding in plain sight

The secrets of green aren't really secrets. What you need to know is right in front of you.

You wouldn't dump your trash on your neighbor's porch, but your company might be putting its trash in your neighbors' lungs. You'd never think of chopping up your kitchen table for firewood to heat your house, yet our industries continue to erode irreplaceable natural capital to support short-term operating benefits. The laws of nature offer the fundamental truths—secrets hiding in plain sight—that business has historically overlooked and now needs to learn. Quickly.

Why do we ignore what we already know?—We're creatures of habit, and it's time to change the habits that no longer serve us. We're used to thinking about waste with an "out of sight, out of mind" attitude, when, in fact, there is no "away." We believe in "waste" when in reality, it has no meaning in nature (see Truth 11, "Waste? Not! Eliminating non-product").

Our accounting systems leave us groping in the dark. Clean air has no monetary value, but try living well without it (see Truth 46, "Reality-based accounting").

What you need to know—The secrets—for successful ecosystems *and* successful businesses—are hiding in plain sight. Nature's living systems, from individual organisms to complex ecosystems, have accumulated 3.85 billion years of evolutionary "research and development" experience in creating and operating complex, efficient, resilient, and adaptive systems. (You see this theme echoed through the rest of this book.) Why should industry reinvent the wheel, I wonder, when the R&D has already been done?

It's time for business people—however urban, however technological—to understand the laws of nature. You wouldn't drive a

> Nature's living systems, from individual organisms to complex ecosystems, have accumulated 3.85 billion years of evolutionary "research and development" experience....

car without knowing the traffic laws, so think about nature's laws before you start taking stuff from it or putting stuff into it. (Like that old poster said: "Gravity. It Isn't Just a Good Idea. It's the Law."[1]) There is a lot about nature we don't yet know, but the basics are not a mystery. Whether it's a meadow or forest, a pond or a desert,

...think about nature's laws before you start taking stuff from it or putting stuff into it.

a business or a national economy, to be sustainable, systems should be renewable, cyclical, edible, and diverse (see Truth 27, "Design with nature").

The Natural Step (TNS) management framework provides one of the most elegant and practical approaches to putting these principles into practice, with four "systems conditions" for sustainability that a provide simple—and testable—compass (which is nothing more than a tool to tell you which direction you're headed). According to TNS (which has been used with great success by hundreds of European companies and dozens of U.S. companies), a sustainable company—or society—must

■ Eliminate the progressive buildup in the biosphere of substances extracted from the Earth's crust (for example, heavy metals and fossil fuels).

■ Eliminate the progressive buildup in the biosphere of chemicals and compounds produced by society (for example, dioxins, PCBs, and DDT).

■ Eliminate the progressive physical degradation and destruction of nature and natural processes (for example, over harvesting forests and paving over critical wildlife habitat).

■ Eliminate conditions that undermine people's capacity to meet their basic human needs (for example, unsafe working conditions and not enough pay to live on).[2]

What you need to do—I realize they never taught you this in business school, but it's time for you to understand the laws of nature. Remember, you wouldn't drive a car without knowing the traffic laws, so why run a business in ignorance of how the world really works? With that basic understanding in hand, you can

- Design with nature—create products, services, and processes that adhere to nature's design principles.
- Buy the right stuff from suppliers—what you buy determines how much waste you make (see Truth 30, "Supply chain management and partnerships").
- Use the Natural Step framework to help make green strategic decisions and to vet your current activities.

These approaches can help you:

- Reduce operating costs and environmental risk
- Get ahead of regulatory frameworks (see Truth 8, "Green regulations")
- Enhance your standing among stakeholders (see Truth 41, "Engaging stakeholders")
- Incorporate environmental concerns into your workplace
- Differentiate your products and services and build a positive brand image

Build awareness of these natural principles into every job function, and teach executive teams, management, and staff how to think about the secrets hiding in plain sight. This is the key to successful implementation (see Truth 40, "Engaging employees"). The good news, as Natural Step founder Karl-Henrik Robèrt is fond of observing, "You already know this."

TRUTH

10

Eco-efficiency:
Good for business and the
environment

What if furniture packages were a centimeter smaller? That's what IKEA executives asked when looking for opportunities to improve efficiency and decrease costs in its supply chain.

The inquiry supported to IKEA's signature flat packaging and led to big financial savings because more products could be shipped with the same number of trucks. This initiative, motivated by material cost savings, resulted in decreased fuel costs and greenhouse gas emissions.[1]

Doing less, better—*Eco-efficiency* means improving environmental quality, efficiency, and profitability by reducing unnecessary inputs and outputs in production and operations—what architect and inventor Buckminster Fuller called "doing more with less." It can include energy efficiency, water conservation, waste minimization, process reengineering, design for environment—and the systematic integration of all of these. It provides a strategic focus that makes sense—for company, region, and nation.

The cost of the waste you make—Your business, regardless of size or sector, uses energy and materials, and produces product and non-product. (Non-product—a term I learned from Bruce Cranford of the DOE—is a better name for waste, emissions, effluent, and pollution.) The business logic for eliminating, not just reducing "waste," is clear: Don't pay for more resources than you need; get the greatest yield from those resources that you can; and stop making product you don't sell (see Truth 11, "Waste? Not! Eliminating non-product").

Eco-efficiency is one of many places where business logic and environmental logic connect. Population growth and rising consumer demand in rapidly developing nations such as India and China put pressure on resource availability and pricing, and corresponding pressure on nature's services (see Truth 9, "Secrets hiding in plain sight"). Consumer demand and resource prices have been knocked back for now by the global recession, but the historic trends are clear. For business to thrive under these constraints, it must do more with less—increasing the value it delivers while decreasing waste, energy use, and material consumption.

A dollar saved is a dollar earned, and other natural laws—The model for efficiency comes directly from nature's billions of years of R&D. The rich interconnection, resilience, and tight, rapid feedback that we find in living systems provide a model of efficiency for industrial systems. These systems are productive, resilient, and adaptive, powered by renewable energy, produce persistent toxic materials only rarely, and operate without "waste"—because the "waste" of any one organism is food for another.

Efficiency is always a good first step in greening your company because it reduces both waste and cost. For example, when clients are thinking about investing in the latest solar panels, we always tell them to invest in energy efficiency first because that both puts money in their pockets and reduces the size of the solar system they need to buy.

Eco-efficiency has many dimensions. The World Business Council on Sustainable Development offers a great guide[2] on where to look for process improvement opportunities:

■ Reduce the material intensity of goods or services

■ Reduce the energy intensity of goods or services

■ Reduce dispersion of toxic materials

■ Improve recyclability (to which I'd add "closed loop processes")

■ Maximum use of renewable resources

■ Greater durability of products

■ Increase service intensity of goods and services

An investment, not a cost—Make the case for eco-efficiency in terms your managers or shareholders can understand. *Return on investment (ROI)*—operating savings divided by the investment needed to generate those savings—generally speaks much more powerfully than "years to payback."

Turning the ROI equation on its side, dividing potential operating savings by your target ROI (or "capital hurdle rate"), gives you the capital expense budget that you have to work with—and that your CFO will accept—to realize those benefits. Improving efficiency has such an attractive ROI that it should be a fundamental part of any company's green strategy.

So why is efficiency sometimes a tough sell in the boardroom? Often energy, resources, and waste management costs seem small relative to other costs (though this will change as energy and carbon prices rise), so efficiency projects can get ignored in favor of bigger fish. But these are costs that are under your control—that *can* be reduced, and often profitably. The solution: Present a clear business case that includes all costs and benefits, including impacts on other parts of the business (see Truth 46, "Reality-based accounting") and their direct impact on the bottom line.

Another obstacle is fear of the potential effects of process changes on productivity or product quality. In our experience, this is a false dichotomy; in fact, we guarantee our clients that we will never recommend efficiency improvements that sacrifice quality, safety, or other key business concerns.

Next steps—Engage your workforce and get them on board—and you'll have more eyes and ears discovering efficiency opportunities. Strive for continuous improvement in efficiency—the Japanese call this kaizen. Remember, no matter how good you are, you can always do better—or your competitors might. Yesterday's "impossible" can become tomorrow's "taken for granted." A continuous improvement approach can keep your eyes open to new technologies and practices and also help increase the chances of a successful efficiency program. Not every efficiency effort works flawlessly, and some need extra tweaking. Instead of casting it aside because "it didn't work last time," improve it!

- Measure and track your efficiency.
- Use EcoAudits to identify facility level opportunities to increase efficiency.
- Combine eco-efficiency with lean process improvement efforts; if you haven't discovered "lean" yet, green can be a good way to start (see Truth 13, "Running lean and green").

TRUTH

11

Waste? Not! Eliminating non-product

When are we going to get as smart as a chicken? When a chicken makes a chicken, the only "wastes" are manure, carbon dioxide, water vapor and methane, and eggshell. But these are all food—for soil, plants, and chickens. Zero waste. Can't industrial society get that smart?

The Price of Everything... From a green business perspective, "wastes" are products that companies "manufacture"—incurring costs, yet adding no value to either customers or shareholders. In fact, "wastes" often cost a business money to dispose of or treat. Spending that money, whether to produce "waste" or treat it, makes no sense—economically or ecologically.

When are we going to get as smart as a chicken?

From an ecological perspective, "zero waste" strategies would better align the human economy with the multigigayears experience of natural systems, where "waste" doesn't exist because the waste of one organism is inevitably the food of another.

I'd go farther, and argue that "waste" has no intrinsic meaning; just as a "weed" isn't a particular type of plant but a plant out of place, "waste" isn't a particular kind of material, but a material out of place. (That's why the Natural Logic stylebook insists we always put the word in quotes—as a reminder that "there ain't no such thing!")

...And the value of zero—"Waste" might be a concept without meaning, but it's a concept with a huge cost. Our "Throughput Pie" graphically presents the ratio of product to Non-Product Output (NPO)—and if a picture is worth a thousand words, this picture is often

"Waste" isn't a particular kind of material, but a material out of place.

worth millions of dollars. I've found few executives who know what the ratio for their company is—and their eyes pop out of their heads when we show them. The ratio for the U.S. economy as a whole is 6 percent product and 94 percent non-product.[1] Your mileage might vary, but I'll bet the ratio is worse—far worse—than you might expect.

What you need to know—What's your Total Cost of Waste (TCOW)? Consider the material purchases that became waste, energy, water, and labor used to process those materials, and such, and the total is typically four to 25 times the disposal fees.[2]

What's your acceptable level of waste? Why?

What's your acceptable level of "waste"? And why? DuPont found it easier to go from a 70 percent waste reduction target to a goal of zero waste, zero injuries, and zero defects than it was to set the initial target. Dupont got so good at eliminating waste—and doing it profitably—that it now offers waste reduction services to supply chains partners and generates a quarter of a billion dollars annually doing so.[3]

What would zero waste look like at *your* company? How would you get there? For whom could *your* "waste" become food?

Reducing—and eliminating—NPO—There are two main strategies to staunch the flow of NPO: Stop making it through efficiency and design innovation; or turn your non-product into product by finding customers for whom your "waste" is their "food." Who can turn your non-product output into their valued input? How?

1. **Look for it!**— "If you can't see the waste, you can't get rid of it." Tony Manos, a lean enterprise consultant, suggests taking teams on "Waste Walks" (see Truth 12, "EcoAudits can guide your course") to look for material wastes and process waste. Never settle for the "'we *have* to do it this way' answer," he says. "There is always room for improvement."[4]

2. **Reduce waste. Process efficiency**—Whether through pollution prevention, waste minimization, business process reengineering, design for environment,[5] or any of a dozen other approaches, most businesses can discover significant-to-vast opportunities to improve production efficiencies. This can be done, for example, through redesign and respecification of products, processes, and equipment (see Truth 10, "Eco-efficiency: Good for business and the environment").

3. **Waste as feedstock: Internal and external cascades**—Cascades that flow the "wastes" of one process into the inputs of another can increase net yields. Internal cascades include cycling scraps back into the product stream, or cogeneration systems cascading

waste heat from electrical generation to heat water. External cascades might start as simple recycling efforts and mature into regional waste exchanges, industrial clusters with symbiotic material, energy needs, and even eco-industrial parks.

4. **Make it tasty: Shift waste chemistry**—*Design* your non-product! Make it something more "digestible" by a hungry industrial mouths down the food chain, and—lo and behold—it's become a product. If no one wants it enough to pay for it or take it off your hands, at least design your non-product to be edible, without harm, by Earth's living systems (see Truth 24, "Biomimcry—learning from life," as well as Truths 25-28).

5. **Break the addiction to "stuff"**—It might go against the economistic tradition of "more stuff means more money," but the value equation of the future will be "produce more value with less physical throughput." Dematerialize your products to get more done with less stuff (see Truth 22, "Product to service").

6. **Measure what matters**—Use business performance metrics to aim toward the right goal; track resource efficiency (resource use or waste generation per unit of product), and throughput efficiency (see Truth 42, "Keeping score").

What next?

■ Check out Taiichi Ohno's "Eight Great Wastes,"[5] and the five that Chauncey Bell adds to Ohno's list.[6]

■ Some decision makers listen to advisors who say, "Zero emissions? Impossible." Fortunately, some operate by a more interesting motto: The difficult we do immediately. The impossible takes a little bit longer.

So, what does *your* throughput pie look like? If a chicken can do "zero waste," maybe you can, too.

TRUTH

12

EcoAudits can guide your course

An EcoAudit is a systematic assessment of your organization's operations—an integrated analysis of resource use that identifies opportunities to improve performance, reduce impact, and save money.

When Auberge Resorts, a luxury hospitality company, asked Natural Logic to help reduce its environmental impacts, we started with EcoAudits—the perfect tool for a company committed to superior guest experience to optimize the performance of its facilities and find thousands of dollars in potential savings.

How will you know if you don't look?—At Auberge, opportunities included simple technical solutions such as making sure lights turn off automatically when guests aren't in a room, more complex ones such as upgrading HVAC systems, and behavioral solutions such as training staff to not overuse cleaning chemicals. Some efficiency assessments focus on a single resource flow; an *integrated* EcoAudit examines the interactions of energy, solid waste, water, air quality, and materials safety, as well as their individual impacts. After performing hundreds of EcoAudits in a wide range of industries, we've found that even the best-run businesses leave money on the table and generate unnecessary environmental impact by running facilities that are inefficient, either because of the equipment they use or how they operate, or both.

EcoAudits help you get the most out of your investments. When you know where you stand, you can make decisions on how to improve your operations—such as making sure equipment you've already paid for is running at peak efficiency. Businesses often pay so much to run old equipment that efficient replacements can pay for themselves.

How to conduct an EcoAudit—You can conduct an EcoAudit with internal staff or hire an outside firm to do it for you. Here are the steps, in either case:

1. **Collect baseline data**—Gather basic information about the facilities—the departments or functions performed, floor area, number of employees, and duty cycles for the building (time/day of use). Collect a year (or ideally two or three years) of energy, water and wastewater, solid waste, and recycling bills to provide a baseline for comparison. Identify or estimate the activities and

locations that generate the major costs and impacts (see Truth 42, "Keeping score").

2. **Perform a walk-through examination**—Evaluate at least one example of each major use-type (for example, offices, production lines, warehouses, guest rooms, lavatories, and laboratories) and walk through your basic business process, following the flow from receiving inputs to shipping products. Observe actions, equipment, and decisions. For example, at what point does a "material" become a "waste"?

Facilities and equipment:

■ **Climate control**—Are HVAC systems efficient, up to date, and properly maintained? Is insulation in roof and walls adequate? Are seals and weatherstripping for doors and windows—including refrigerator door seals—adequate and in good shape? Are appropriate load management strategies in use? Record capacity (hp, W, Btuh, cfm, tons cooling, and such).

■ **Lighting**—Create a lighting census. How many lamps, of what type and wattage, in which locations? (It's often easier to find wattage information in the supply closet instead of climbing up to ceiling fixtures.)

■ **Motors and appliances**—Record faceplate data and approximate duty cycles for motors, electrical equipment, and appliances, and compare efficiency with current models.

■ **Load management**—Check load-shifting practices, such as use of occupancy sensors and set-back thermostats, doing laundry in off-peak hours, or watering the landscaping in the early morning.

■ **Water**—Check faucets and toilets for leaks and flow rates (and dishwashers for temperature settings); ensure they meet or exceed current efficiency standards—1.6 gallons per flush toilets, 1.5 gallon per minute faucets in my neck of the woods at the time of this writing; check your local listings.[1]

Processes:

■ **Equipment use**—Even efficient equipment has to be operated correctly. Ensure that lights aren't on where not needed, low-flow faucets don't run unnecessarily, and that HVAC systems deliver proper temperatures at the proper times.

- **Waste and recycling**—Are recycling and compost bins present? If so, do occupants use them? Estimate percentage of waste by type (metals, plastics, paper, organics, and so on) and let people know how much they throw away.

- **Materials**—Are paper, equipment, and cleaning supplies eco-efficient, with a high-percentage of recycled, nontoxic material. Buy smart because your purchases determine your "wastes" (see Truth 29, "Environmentally preferable purchasing").

Engage employees along the way. Ask people about what they do and why they do it that way. The people who do the work often have ideas on how to improve it—and their buy-in is critical for getting recommendations adopted (see Truth 40, "Engaging employees").

3. Put the data to work.

- List the opportunities. Your observations will generate numerous ideas for efficiency improvement, such as lighting upgrades, new equipment, better insulation, and waste-reducing practices.

- Evaluate opportunities. Estimate cost, impacts, and benefits for each opportunity. Use life-cycle costing, considering costs and benefits over the lifetime of the measure, not just first costs. Use percentage return on investment (ROI), not years to payback, which often leaves profitable projects on the back burner.

- Prioritize opportunities. Our clients prioritize options based on ROI, ease of implementation, scale of impact, or a combination. Engage decision makers before you start the process, and plan with their needs in mind; ROI rankings typically speak to managers with budget responsibility, whereas ease of implementation may be critical to floor managers.

- Communicate your recommendations. Many of your findings depend on behavior change, so present them in a way that suits the audience. We've seen formal reports, lunchtime presentations, and even signage—such as labeling trash bins "landfill"—work effectively.

- Train workers and stakeholders in the new practices that you recommend. If the changes are inconvenient, they're unlikely to stick. On the other hand, we've seen workers readily adopt additional tasks when they're recognized for their efforts.

Recognition can go farther than financial incentives (see Truth 43, "Employee incentives").

■ Track your results. Calculate the percentage change against baselines, in dollars, kWh, tons, and gallons.

■ Follow up. Check in with managers and staff a few weeks or months later to see which recommendations work and what needs further adjustment.

Look small to see big—Start with a mini-audit of your office, floor, or home. Make a list of things to check, record what needs to be improved, and discuss your findings with your colleagues.

As you perform an informal EcoAudit, you can learn to spot inefficiencies such as lights being left on or windows being left open while air conditioners are running. EcoAudits can be continual. Learn to look for opportunities every day.

TRUTH

13

Running lean and green

Leaders at Toyota Motor Corporation developed a philosophy and method for building cars that has become a legendary model for lean production systems. Toyota set about "making the vehicles ordered by customers in the quickest and most efficient way, in order to deliver the vehicles as quickly as possible" by eliminating stress on the system, which reduces inconsistencies in production and, therefore, eliminates waste.[1] The resulting Toyota Production System (TPS) was wildly successful and has been emulated and studied all over the world. A key reason for its success is that it embeds continuous improvement into the company's culture and practices.

What is lean and green?—The next step is the marriage of lean and green. "Green" provides a vision and goals, while "lean" provides the system for effective implementation. "Lean"—whether lean manufacturing, lean accounting, or lean anything—is more than cost cutting through efficiency; it's about creating a culture that consistently finds new opportunities to improve efficiency and environmental performance, and feedback systems that streamline and improve business operations and reduce your company's impact on the environment.

Why it's important—Increasing efficiency and reducing waste don't just happen on their own. You need a systematic plan to get managers and workers to implement goals. Lean practices help achieve this. By being lean *and* green, you can increase profit by building this process of cutting waste and reducing risk into the daily practice of your company.

The waste you know—In developing the TPS, Toyota executive Taiichi Ohno identified seven essential types of waste, or "muda:"[2]

- **Defects**—Errors in production
- **Over-production**—Making more than is needed
- **Conveyance**—Excess transportation
- **Waiting**—Delays in production and delivery of product
- **Inventory**—Excess materials or product not being used or sold
- **Motion**—Unnecessary actions in production process

- **Overprocessing**—Training for tasks not performed, developing unnecessary features

Other candidates you might consider for the list of wastes: energy and water use, non-product (pollution), untapped human potential, and inappropriate systems. Consider my colleague Chauncey Bell's provocative "Five Great Wastes" as well:[3] Not Listening, Bureaucratic Styles, Worship of Information, Suppressing Innovation, and Work as Toil.

Design waste out of your business with lean methods—Lean operations are built on a foundation of continual improvement (kaizen in Japanese), with the intent that teams will not only improve efficiency once but continue to systematically find opportunities to do so. Here are some tools for embedding kaizen into your company. (The metaphor is manufacturing, but lean can apply to any aspect of any business.) But keep in mind: You won't learn this from a book (even a longer book than this one!), without human interaction and deep respect.

- Use jidoka, or "automation with a human touch." When a problem occurs, the process stops immediately, preventing defective products from being produced, and the issue is communicated on a central problem display board. Feedback is key—lean systems run on information provided throughout the production chain, not a traditional "one-way" signal. The "voice of the customer"— internal and external—guides members of your supply chain to continue producing, stop, speed up, or slow down. Proceeding without the authority of this signal can result in waste from stockpiling supplies downstream from your own operation.

- Consider "just in time" operations. Make only what is needed, when it is needed, and in the amount needed. This is also called "pull production" because products and materials are produced when the downstream party requests them, instead of being pushed by the producer. It can improve utilization and flow, and cut waste, inventory (considered a liability in lean, not an asset, as in traditional accounting), and set-up times.

- Level out the workload to avoid stress on workers and the production system, which can lead to suboptimal performance and lapses in quality. One way to do this is to make products in smaller batches using "cellular manufacturing"—where adaptable and mobile teams can work on what's needed—instead of the traditional approach of creating large batches for "economy of scale" and waiting for orders.

Lean is more than knowledge about the preceding methods. People are the key to the process, and they need to be united in their awareness, acceptance, and participation of a lean production culture; that's why it's been so hard for Detroit to copy Toyota's success. Innovation is more likely when you integrate teams and solicit every worker's input on how to continuously improve. For example, manufacturing employees hold process knowledge that environment health and safety teams need to improve conditions by removing hazards and other wastes, including the Three M's that lean manufacturing targets:

- **Muri**—Overburden, relieved by standardized work sequences
- **Mura**—Inconsistency, resolved by quickly identifying irregularities in parts
- **Muda**—Waste, removed by only producing goods and services that are needed (and only in the amounts needed)

Green provides a frame and a vision for the techniques of lean; lean provides disciplined methodology for embedding green into daily business practice.

The lean process doesn't end. Strive for constant improvement. Measure your progress so that you know what's working and what needs adjusting.

Go and see for yourself—Green provides a frame and a vision for the techniques of lean; lean provides disciplined methodology for embedding green into daily business practice. How can you put them together in your organization?

TRUTH

14

Carbon footprinting

Where do you start if your company wants to decrease its impact on climate change? Should you decrease the amount of fossil fuels your employees use to get to work? Or maybe the way you ship your product is more important. Maybe you should launch a companywide energy-efficiency campaign. What about the greenhouse gases in manufacturing processes? Carbon footprinting is a powerful tool for helping you figure out where to start.

A carbon footprint is the measure of the greenhouse gases (GHGs) produced by a given activity, product, business, or supply chain, expressed in tons of carbon dioxide equivalents (the standard unit for describing carbon dioxide emissions). Carbon footprints are used to measure the impact that businesses, products, people, and events have on climate change. The six primary greenhouse gases— carbon dioxide, nitrous oxide, methane, HFCs, PFCs, and SF6—have varying impacts on climate change, so they are expressed as carbon equivalents to enable comparison of impact. For example, a ton of methane has 21 times the climate impact of a ton of carbon, whereas a ton of SF_6 (Sulfur Hexafluoride) has 23,900 times the impact.

Measure what matters the most—As businesses and regulators set goals for reducing their impacts on the climate, they need clear data to track progress and a common language for talking about data. Carbon footprints provide a common language to talk about combating climate change.

The first step in reducing your company's impact on climate change is to know how much you're contributing and where those contributions come from. Knowing your carbon footprint also lowers your risk in the face of upcoming carbon regulation and trading schemes, and the growing scrutiny that pension funds and other large investors are giving to impacts of GHG emissions on company performance and forward risk (see Truth 15, "Reducing your carbon footprint," and Truth 48, "Carbon trading and offsets").

Knowing your carbon footprint, according to Kyle Tanger, president of Clear Carbon Consulting (a Natural Logic ally), allows you to

- Identify and prioritize efficiency improvements.
- Evaluate various GHG reduction strategies.
- Measure progress toward sustainability goals.

- Report corporate carbon position to senior management, shareholders, and voluntary reporting initiatives (like the Carbon Disclosure Project or the California Climate Registry).

- Develop strategies that encompass design, management, reduction, and trading, and integrate these with your business strategy.

Know how to determine your footprint—There are two key phases in determining your carbon footprint.

Phase 1: Define your footprint

- Set boundaries. A carbon footprint must include direct emissions, from sources you own or control, such as fuel combustion from boilers and company-owned vehicles (Scope 1); indirect emissions, from your consumption of electricity, steam, or heat produced by another organization (Scope 2); and might include supply-chain emissions, from sources (such as air travel) not owned or controlled by the company but that are a consequence of company activity (Scope 3). Most companies start with Scopes 1 and 2. You need Scope 3 to get a full understanding of impacts and opportunities, but getting the data is a more challenging task. (For more information about scope definitions and categories, check out the Greenhouse Gas Protocol at www. ghgprotocol.org.)

- Determine and measure a baseline year. You'll be comparing future years' performance against this year.

- Know which activities contribute to your footprint. These might include fuel burned in furnaces, boilers, generators, water heaters, and company-owned vehicles; waste decomposition; and gaseous losses of CFCs and HCFCs from chillers, refrigerators, and air conditioners, and SF6 from electrical equipment.

Phase 2: Quantify your footprint

- Identify where your relevant data is. Who has it—or knows where the appropriate data lives? Data sources commonly include fuel invoices (Scope 1) and energy bills (Scope 2).

- Identify people at your company who know how to get hold of that data.

- Collect data and identify the gaps in your data.

- If invoices for some months are missing, for instance, it's not the end of the world; you can extrapolate from data available (make sure to document your assumptions) and plan to eliminate the gaps next year.

- Analyze your data and convert your gallons of fuel, electricity purchased, and so on into GHG equivalents so that you can compare "apples to apples" and add them up. You can use conversion factors in carbon footprint calculators or from other established resources.

- Survey your facilities and operations to identify opportunities to drive down your footprint in the most impactful and financially beneficial ways.

- Analyze and report your findings. You can use the report internally, or publish it through EPA's Climate Leaders or the Carbon Disclosure Project.

Be sure to communicate your findings effectively, whether to your customers, employees, or investment analysts—and be aware that each audience is getting more interested. Report findings in context—tons per unit of revenue, product, or facility—as well as in absolute tons; for some audiences, you might want to use comparisons such as "that's the same amount of carbon that 1,000 cars emit in a year."

Know the tools of the trade. There's a rapidly growing array of tools, methods, and resources out there that can help your efforts. Collections of tools and emission factors are available from WRI, Climate Leaders, the U.S. Department of Energy, and the Intergovernmental Panel on Climate Change (IPCC). You can try out some online carbon calculators at the collection I've built: www.squidoo.com/carboncalcs.

The right yardstick for the job—Now you have a lot of data. How will you put it to use? Here's how:

1. Understand the emissions sources in your organization (and supply chain).

2. Determine the biggest contributors to your carbon footprint.

3. Identify and prioritize opportunities to reduce it (see Truth 15).

4. Systematically reduce your footprint—including your Scope 3 emissions—even if you don't plan on formally reporting them.

5. Consider the future market value of emissions reductions as market-based cap and trade systems or carbon taxes come into play.

6. Trade your emissions.

7. As a last resort, offset your remaining footprint.

8. Finally, think about how to streamline and integrate carbon footprinting into your normal business process in coming years.

TRUTH

15

Reducing your
carbon footprint

Okay, you've determined your carbon footprint and reported it in the relevant disclosure programs. Now it's time to put your business on a low-carbon diet, and reduce that footprint—strategically and profitably. Reducing your carbon emissions strategically can make the changes easier to implement and more likely to work. Reducing them profitably can help your bottom line, now and in the future. The need to reduce dramatically greenhouse gas emissions is clear. Without major shifts in the way we do business, the future of business itself—as well as the future of the climate—is at risk.

Carbon is going to start costing you money, or making you money. You choose. Governments are now developing carbon markets, carbon taxes, and other economic incentives for businesses to reduce their emissions. Operations such as shipping and transportation will have added costs—and shipping efficiently will have added value.

That means you'll need to know:

- Where your emissions come from
- Which emissions are most significant
- Which emissions are most readily reducible
- How you need to change processes and materials to reduce emissions
- How to reduce emissions profitably
- What your competitors are doing about their carbon emissions

How to put your business on a low-carbon diet—Use these tips to help reduce your carbon footprint:

- **Estimate your baseline emissions**—Knowing where you currently stand can help you set meaningful reduction goals and target high-leverage opportunities for reduction (see Truth 14, "Carbon footprinting").
- **Set goals**—There are two types of goals for carbon reductions: absolute reductions (tons of CO_2 equivalents, or CO_2e) and intensity reductions (for example, tons of CO_2e per dollar of profit) (see Truth 7, "How green is good enough?").

- **Identify priority reduction opportunities**—Which activities have the largest climate impacts? Which are most easily addressable? Evaluate your alternatives. Address those activities in this order:

  1. Maximize efficiency.
  2. Replace remaining fossil energy with renewable energy.
  3. Trade or offset remaining carbon emissions.

  Efficiency is usually your most cost-effective tool to slash emissions. Make sure your facilities are energy efficient, consolidate shipping, and minimize material wastes. Trading and offsetting should be the last steps, not the first.

- **Rethink and reengineer**—How can you provide equivalent or even additional value to your customers with lower carbon intensity? There is a common myth that "environment" is an added cost—but the truth is designing with the environment in mind opens doors to new innovations, more efficient practices, and new markets, often at *lower* cost.

Where to look for reduction opportunities—Most organizations have many opportunities to reduce their carbon emissions. Because those emissions are generally connected to energy use, reductions can be profitable as well. With one recent client, we identified opportunities to cut emissions by 14 percent—with a 37 percent ROI. Here are just a few examples:

- Scope 1: Reduce direct emissions from fuel combustion.

  - Check settings and hours of operation of boilers and heating systems.
  - Properly insulate your building.
  - Purchase fleet vehicles with high fuel economy, and keep them well maintained.
  - Reduce hot water use.

- Scope 2: Reduce indirect emissions from grid-purchased electricity.

  - Maximize your energy efficiency. Harvest "low hanging fruit" by upgrading to efficient lighting, air conditioning, motors, and computer equipment.
  - Buy renewable energy from your local utility.
  - Generate electricity from onsite renewable energy sources, such as fuel cells, wind, solar, and other renewables.

- Consider installing cogeneration (or combined heat and power [CHP]) systems where there are opportunities to get multiple benefits (generating electricity onsite and using the "waste" heat to meet heating and cooling needs) from each dollar of energy spend.

- Scope 3: Scan your supply chain for opportunities to reduce indirect emissions that you don't directly control.
  - Ask your suppliers for *their* carbon emissions data—as Wal-Mart is doing—and choose low carbon options.
  - Source local materials. Less shipping often reduces your supply chain carbon impact—but only if the local producer is efficient.
  - Set up efficient shipping operations.
  - Buy recycled materials. Creating products with virgin materials is more energy-intensive than using recycled material.

Next steps—After you identify reductions, follow these steps to start making progress:

1. After you identify your list of opportunities for carbon reductions, prioritize the list based on ROI and ease of implementation. Changing light bulbs is easier than upgrading your fleet, but priorities will differ among companies. If you're already shopping for new vehicles, it's a perfect time to buy smarter. Presenting the ROI of efficiency measures can help make the financial case to decision makers.

2. Create an implementation plan. Set schedules for necessary adjustments, define roles and responsibilities, and train your staff on new practices, vendors, or supplies.

3. Measure your performance. Use your emission baseline to see how well your efforts are working. Always think about and talk about your emissions reductions in context, as ratios and trends, and total tonnage.

4. Communicate progress clearly. Vague claims can raise legal issues and hurt you in the marketplace; clear communications can help employees, investors, and customers understand your reductions.

TRUTH

16

Green branding and messaging

What image or idea comes to mind when you think of Clif Bar, Patagonia, or General Electric? They all project a green image. A company creates a green brand and message when it ties its identity to its impacts on the environment. The green message can tell a story about how raw materials are harvested from the environment, how the company measures its impact on the environment, or even how the company draws inspiration from the environment.

Your brand is the story of who you are—for internal and external markets. Putting your story at the forefront of your employees' minds can help drive you toward sustainability. The value of a company's brand is often greater than the value of tangible assets; one KPMG study found that more than 55 percent of a company's share value is a function of *intangibles*, such as brand and reputation. Green messaging can be a powerful way to differentiate your company and product; for example, Seventh Generation markets nontoxic cleaning products, soaps, detergents, and toilet paper—goods that consumers often see as indistinguishable commodities; Seventh Generation stands out not only because it claims that its products are safe and environmentally responsible, but also because it communicates its distinctive story—and integrity— through packaging, advertising, and word of mouth.

Green messaging can be a powerful way to differentiate your company and product.

Green messaging is also potentially a way to get into trouble when marketing is disconnected from reality. Consumers quickly identify and react negatively to greenwashing campaigns that overstate or misrepresent green claims (see Truth 18, "Green marketing claims"), such as SUVs marketed as green despite their meager fuel efficiency. Because the leaders among green consumers (see Truth 19, "Reaching conscious consumers") tend to communicate with each other about green products (in person and on the Internet), they can have a strong, widespread, and negative influence when they feel that a company misleads.

Create a compelling green message—What makes a compelling green message? The best green messages—like any other compelling messages—tell the truth, convey quality, and relate to matters that your customers believe affect them directly. Most customers aren't willing to sacrifice quality and functionality for green, so green messaging works best when it enhances rather than replaces a product's basic value.

Know how to express your message—and be innovative! Stonyfield Farms, the world's leading organic yogurt producer, turned its green messaging into free public relations, with a roadside Tire Inflation Station to show its commitment to sustainability. (Cars with inflated tires get better gas mileage, consume less fuel, and thus emit fewer greenhouse gasses.) Stonyfield received free news coverage and shared its message with the world. Green messaging also has a powerful presence in word of mouth and the blogosphere.

Which media outlets should you use? All the above! Make green messaging part of a consistent, integrated approach, and back it up with action.

Creating your green message and branding—Here are a few elements of crafting a credible green message for your business:

- **Do your homework**—Study other companies that have successfully leveraged green messaging.

- **Look in the mirror**—Examine your own business to see if any of your practices are inconsistent with a green message—and if so, change them. (The practices, not the messaging!)

> Establish credibility with actions that back up your message. Say little, and do much.

- **Communicate your values**—Messaging is all about communication, and green messaging is about sharing your values with consumers.

- **Establish credibility with actions that back up your message**—Say little, and do much. If you keep at it, build a history of green messaging, and back up your words with actions, you can outlast the green wannabees and stand out in the crowd.

- **Experiment publicly**—Many companies have great green programs but are reluctant to go public about them for fear of attracting added scrutiny. If your message is strong and your work is good, you should be in the clear.

- **Tell the truth**—Integrity matters to this market, as it should for us all, so play it straight. Besides, as Mark Twain famously said, "If you tell the truth, you don't have to remember anything."

TRUTH

17

Creating strong EcoLabels

Eco-friendly. Green. Organic. Made with organic materials. Recycled. Recyclable. All-natural. Free-range. Cruelty-free. The market for environmentally sound products is booming, but going to the store can leave you and your customers in a green cloud of confusion. More products carry environmental claims on their packaging, but it's not always clear what they mean. EcoLabels are an attempt to standardize and clearly communicate the environmental impacts of a product to consumers.

EcoLabels and standards not only protect consumers, but they also protect conscious producers by preventing free-riders from diluting their position with bogus claims. EcoLabels also provide certainty and stability to the market. Just as Underwriters Laboratory provides a respected product safety standard, the USDA Organic label assures consumers that they're actually getting an organic product.

EcoLabels are great communication tools. When a label is established, it provides companies with a simplified way to communicate their environmental credentials. When a company says its product is certified USDA Organic, many customers recognize the label and immediately know what it means.

EcoLabels drive markets toward sustainability by giving companies a standard to which to aim. When a company tells its customers that its facility is certified LEED Platinum, other companies feel competitive pressure to reach the same standard.

Some of the most common and well-defined EcoLabels in the United States include the following:

- **USDA Organic**—Agricultural and food products
- **U.S. EPA Energy Star**—Appliances, office equipment, buildings
- **Forest Stewardship Council Certified**—Forest and timber products
- **Leadership in Energy and Environmental Design (LEED)**—Buildings

Types of EcoLabels—The International Standards Organization (ISO) recognizes three kinds of ecolabels:

- **Seals of approval**—You get the label if you meet the standard.

- **Claims**—Adding terms such as *organic* or *biodegradable* to the product name. This type is the most at risk of greenwashing.

- **Grade**—*USDA choice beef* or *three-star restaurant* graded labels help consumers choose the level of price and quality they prefer.

What makes a good EcoLabel? The strongest EcoLabels are industry-specific, accurate, third-party verified, and describe actions that benefit the environment. Customers more readily trust labels run by nonprofits or governments than those created by industry. A good EcoLabel should also be a marketing asset. A memorable name, a recognizable logo, and a good story can go a long way in communicating the value of the label, while setting it apart in a field crowded by weak environmental claims.

Not all EcoLabels are created equal. In the United States, some EcoLabels are legally defined. For example, when a food company claims that its product is organic, it must document that its product is grown without pesticides, antibiotics, synthetic fertilizers, hormones, or bioengineering. Those claims are subject to third-party verification before the product can wear the USDA Organic label.

The U.S. Federal Trade Commission (FTC) created specific guidelines for EcoLabels, which "should be accompanied by information that explains the basis for the award. If the seal-of-approval implies that a third party has certified the product, the certifying party must be truly independent from the advertiser and must have professional expertise in the area that is being certified."

Other EcoLabels apply to whole industries, products, or components of products. For example, the Forest Stewardship Council (FSC), which certifies sustainable wood products, offers

- **Forest Management certification**—Used for forest or plantation areas

- **Chain of Custody certification**—Used to track certified material from forest to store

- **Controlled Wood certification**—Used to control the noncertified material in certified products to avoid timber from the most destructive and harmful practices

FSC's Chain of Custody certification is an example of a life cycle EcoLabel. *Life cycle labels* signify that a product has been examined throughout its raw material, processing, and sales phases. Other EcoLabels are *single-issue*, which focus on one particular environmental impact, such as a vegetable labeled *pesticide free*.

Businesses can also be certified for EcoLabels. These can be either sector-specific labels, such as *green hotels*, or more generic labels that focus on business operations, such as the *certified green business* label offered by county governments in the San Francisco Bay Area and elsewhere.

Countries differ in their treatment of EcoLabels. The European Union has a standardized EcoLabel, signified by the Eco-Flower logo, which covers a wide range of food and consumer products and takes a life-cycle approach. Germany has the Blue Angel certification, one of the earliest EcoLabels. Canada's EcoLogo is North America's largest environmental standard and certification mark.

Companies have been active, too. British supermarket chain Tesco and other retailers have been working to develop *carbon labels* for food products, while Wal-Mart has been working with suppliers to develop *supplier scorecards*, as part of an internal certification process.

Choosing the right EcoLabel—Here are some things to consider when choosing the right EcoLabel for your product or business:

- Find out if there are EcoLabels that apply to your products, services, or sector. (You can find an exhaustive list of EcoLabels at http://ecolabelling.org.)

- Determine whether your existing products or services are worthy of EcoLabels or could become worthy as you reduce the environmental footprint of your designs and operations.

- Do your homework. Make sure the EcoLabel you're considering is reputable. Consumers (and watchdog groups) are increasingly adept at seeing through "greenwashing."

- No EcoLabels apply to your business? It might make sense to create your own. When the Berkeley, California-based dental office Transcendentist saw that its industry had no green standard, it asked my company, Natural Logic, to help them create the Eco-Dentistry Association.

EcoLabels for small businesses—What about small businesses? EcoLabels might favor larger businesses that have more time and money to devote to the certification process. Some small companies have responded by creating alternate standards, such as *Certified Naturally Grown*. Others, from farmers to builders, choose to meet the standards but skip the certification process, and rely on reputation and word of mouth. Others, particularly in the organic food industry, feel that the EcoLabel is important enough to find ways to make the process work.

TRUTH
18

Green marketing claims

Green marketing claims are statements that companies make in their advertising and messaging that describe green attributes of their products and services. For example, you might pick up two food packages at the store and see the labels "100% Organic" on one and "Eco-friendly" on the other. These both make claims about the products, but they have different meanings and impacts: One has a specific legal definition; the other is so unspecific that many find it misleading.

Buyers have varying affinities for green products (as for many products—that's what makes horse races!), but the bottom line is that green claims appeal to a large and growing constituency that is often willing to pay price premiums for "greener" products (see Truth 19, "Reaching conscious consumers").

Some companies have overstated their green claims and have suffered in the market. Consumer watchdog groups and environmental NGOs (nongovernmental organizations) are on the lookout for misleading or even weak green claims. NGOs often have market muscle—sales of bottled water dropped dramatically when NGOs reported that companies touting the clean and healthy attributes of their water were ignoring climate issues, packaging safety, and waste production.

Inaccurate or overstated green claims can also mislead the market. The collective effect of weak green claims is that it turns people off of green marketing even if a watchdog group isn't pointing fingers. If consumers start tuning out green messages, significant market opportunities will be lost.

Green claims—Know the different types of green claims and where to find them. Know how to recognize and avoid "greenwash." *Greenwashing* is the act of misleading consumers regarding the environmental practices of a company or the environmental benefits of a product or service—even with the best of intentions. The marketing firm Terrachoice published a report called "The 6 Sins of Greenwashing" based on its analysis of green claims; in order of observed frequency:

■ The "sin of the hidden trade-off" occurs when a company makes a green claim on one product attribute, which obscures a less green aspect. For example, if you advertise that your shirt is made of 100 percent organic cotton, but it was processed with toxic dye, this would be considered a hidden trade-off.

- An example of the "sin of no proof" is when companies claim that their products are made in factories with safe working conditions, but consumers have no way of verifying the claim.

- The "sin of vagueness" is commonly seen in recycled materials claims. If a company says it uses "recycled paper," it could mean they recycle scrap material from within the manufacturing process and count that as recycled material. Others use post-consumer recycled material. The best way to avoid vagueness is to be specific—for example, "this product contains 70 percent post-consumer recycled material."

- The "sin of irrelevance." Some companies boast that their product is "CFC-Free" even though all products are, because chlorofluorocarbons were banned in the 1980s. Some products that are completely unrelated to CFCs even carry that meaningless claim, but still mislead consumers.

- The "sin of fibbing" is misleading in a straightforward way. These are claims that are simply false. Lying to your customers is ultimately counterproductive—as well as unethical.

- The "sin of lesser of two evils" occurs when a harmful product is positioned as green, such as organic cigarettes.

Honest claims—With what not to do in mind, a good, clear, green claim should be specific, truthful, verifiable, and meaningful.

Review applicable regulations before launching a green product or marketing campaign. Canada has established guidelines, and the U.S. Federal Trade Commission is reworking its own policies as I write this. ISO standard 14021 covers green claims. Additional legislation is on the way in the United States and in other countries, so be sure you know which claims are legally binding before making those claims. The best policy for your business is to make appropriate, true green claims that are more likely to pass regulatory scrutiny.

...a good, clear, green claim should be specific, truthful, verifiable, and meaningful.

Making green claims—Before you make green product claims, take these steps:

- Assess which of your products and services might deserve green claims.

- Review your company's current green claims to make sure they're sound, legal, and informative to your customer.

- If a labeling or certification scheme (see Truth 17, "Creating strong EcoLabels") doesn't exist, talk to your customers about what aspects of "green" are most important to them.

- If an independent verification system exists for your product (or business), consider the costs and benefits of having your claims formally certified.

TRUTH

19

Reaching conscious
consumers

"Conscious consumers" are a $200 billion market segment of people focused on health and fitness, the environment, personal development, sustainable living, and social justice. The market was first identified by sociologist Paul Ray in his 1995 book, *The Cultural Creatives: How 50 Million People Are Changing the World* (with roots in earlier "psychographic" analysis such as Stanford Research Institute's Values and LifeStyles Survey (VALS).

Now often called LOHAS (Lifestyles of Health and Sustainability), the U.S. market for these goods and services was estimated at $209 billion in the United States in 2005 (the latest comprehensive analysis). Approximately 41 million or 19 percent of U.S. adults were considered LOHAS consumers.[1]

This is a large and growing market—and the LOHAS consumer is often willing to pay a premium for products that represent their values. Just walk into a Whole Foods grocery store and compare what you see to an average grocery—you'll see more information about each product and a wider range of pricing. The market is also growing internationally. The demand for sustainable, healthy, and responsible products is felt in Asia and Europe, especially where natural resources are limited. The Natural Marketing Institute classified 29.3 percent of all Japanese adults as LOHAS consumers.[2] Although the term LOHAS was first introduced to Japan in 2002, 22 percent of the population above the age of 15 recognizes the term.

The most recent estimates describe the U.S. LOHAS market as follows:

- **Personal Health**—Includes natural/organic foods, dietary supplements, natural and organic personal care products, alternative medicine, yoga, health/fitness, and media—$118 billion
- **Green Building**—Includes ENERGY STAR products and homes, other green-certified homes, materials, and solar panels—$50 billion
- **Eco-Tourism**—Includes eco-travel and adventures—$24 billion
- **Natural Lifestyles**—Includes home furnishings/supplies, natural pet products, cleaners, apparel, and philanthropy—$10.6 billion
- **Alternative Vehicles**—Includes hybrid vehicles, biodiesel, and car sharing—$5.8 billion

- **Alternative Energy**—Includes renewable energy, green pricing programs, and renewable energy certificates (RECs)—$380 million

Although the definitions are both loose and debatable, it's clear that each of these segments has grown substantially since 2005—though it's not at all clear what impact the global financial crisis (in full swing as I write this) will have, either on the segments themselves or the willingness to pay premium prices. My guess? Buyers will see some of these segments as luxuries and cut back; other markets will be "stickier." For example, some people are not likely to eat less healthy food, though they might change where they buy it. Secondly, the current global trends are heading in this direction.

Identifying conscious consumers—Conscious consumers come in different shades of green, according to the Natural Market Institute.

- **LOHAS**—Represents the dedicated core of the market; these consumers have a strong inclination to buy products that express their green values, and the strongest willingness to pay more for that expression.
- **Naturalites**—Most concerned with making health-conscious purchases.
- **Drifters**—Purchase green products if they see a direct benefit of doing so.
- **Conventionals**—Practical, motivated by local issues, and are likely to purchase green products when they are presented in mainstream outlets.
- **Unconcerned**—Motivated by low prices and is unlikely to change purchasing habits based on LOHAS values.

The LOHAS/conscious consumer market segment is driving the broader market for sustainable products, which makes it an important force to understand in greening your business. You see it in the way "average" businesses move toward sustainability to reach the LOHAS consumer. When you walk into a supermarket, you often see a section with Whole Foods-type products that advertise their green attributes. The typical profile of a consumer with LOHAS values is changing from a high-income, urban elite into the mainstream, so most people wouldn't think of Wal-Mart and LOHAS in the same phrase; but Wal-Mart's organic cotton yoga clothing sold out as soon as it was introduced because it connected Wal-Mart strength—affordability—with recognition of ever-widening LOHAS concerns.

There are products all around you that appeal to the LOHAS crowd, such as the Toyota Prius, Tom's of Maine toothpaste, alternative medicines, organic foods, and socially responsible investment funds. Taken one at a time, these might not be news; but it is news that these segments are large—and growing—and that big companies are going after them.

Reaching conscious consumers—You need to understand LOHAS concerns, and how they connect with your products and services. If your offerings naturally address LOHAS concerns—or if they could be modified to do so—assess the costs and benefits of pursuing the LOHAS sector.

Study the companies in your sector that position themselves as "green" (whether they're truly walking the talk or just talking the talk). What works for them? Where are your business's potential strengths for this market (whether current unleveraged benefits or potential changes in materials and processes that could enhance your appeal)?

But don't make false, misleading, or even weak claims to the LOHAS crowd. These customers tend to be much more informed than other consumers and have strong word-of-mouth networks (think blogosphere!), so if you lose credibility with a few consumers, the bad news can travel fast.

And consider this: If "everyone" is getting on the green bandwagon, is this really a strategic sector? As the LOHAS sector overlaps more with mainstream consumers, it might become harder to differentiate products based solely on its sustainability and health aspects, when a growing number of companies make those claims. The real power and potential lie not in a marketing-focused "we're green, too—at least a little" approach. The real power and potential is in real innovation that delivers better performance and value for the price—in greening as in everything else.

TRUTH

20

What makes a product green?

If you're a product business, you can't be a green business without green products. (I'll talk about whether you *should* be a product business in Truth 22, "Product to service.") And because the market for green products is large and growing rapidly, offering green products is the right thing to do. But what makes a product green? And what makes it green enough?

You can count on a future with greener products. Common sense could have told you that toxic materials in children's toys were a bad idea, and that sooner or later regulators or consumers would act. Developing green products now can keep you ahead of the game, rather than playing catch-up (see Truth 32, "Clearing the rising bar").

What makes "green" green?—Let's start with the obvious: A "green" product should be "better for the environment." But what does that mean? What criteria should you consider? Is "doing less harm" good enough, or should environmental improvement—restoration and regeneration—be part of the mix?

Is "doing less harm" good enough?

Green products should minimize their impact on the environment over their entire life cycle, from cradle to grave—ideally from cradle to cradle!

Factors to consider include the following:

- Material inputs that comprise the products
- Energy used to extract and ship inputs and products
- Energy, water, and resources used to create the product
- Energy, water, and material use associated with the product's normal use
- Resources used for its disposal or recycling at the end of its useful life
- Environmental and health impacts every step of the way

The ideal green product won't just deliver less impact than "normal" products—it will actually build environmental quality and health (see Truth 7, "How green is good enough?").

Life cycle assessments—Some companies use Life Cycle Assessments (LCA)[1] to help pinpoint where a product's biggest impacts occur, and which performance improvements to prioritize.

Because LCAs are too expensive to do on every product, I recommend "life cycle thinking:"[2]

- Examine your most significant inputs, outputs. and processes.
- Focus first on those with the largest inputs or outputs.
- Identify, for each, the direct impacts of your actions, and the impacts up and down your value chain.
- Consider your options to profitability reduce environmental impacts and increase resilience—for both your company and for the rest of your food chain.

The Natural Step—The simplest set of guiding principles come from The Natural Step (TNS), which is described in more detail in Truth 9, "Secrets hiding in plain sight"). Or simpler still

- Dematerialize.
- Detoxify.
- Get cyclical.
- Go renewable.

When is "green" NOT green?—Some companies still make "green" product claims, when it's clear to everyone else that they're really not green—often more out of ignorance than trying to mislead. To avoid being "that company," avoid these pitfalls:

- Greening gradually is fine, but don't fall for the green trade-off (see Truth 18, "Green marketing claims").
- Don't make claims you can't stand behind. For example, sustainably harvested wood depends on a clear chain of custody, so there is no risk of it being mixed with unsustainably harvested wood.
- Don't ignore your product after it leaves your company. Is it used in a green way? Is it actually recycled? For example, CFL lightbulbs are energy-efficient, but if people put them in the wrong type of fixture, they can burn out quickly, and increase waste and demand for materials.

What's green enough?—That's the question that has to be asked—and that might have no universal answer. Greenness (and specific aspects of green, such as carbon footprint, recycled content, or toxicity) is more important to some customers than others. So build a culture of constant improvement that won't be satisfied with first steps. For example, Patagonia, a leader in green adventure gear, has maintained its leadership by never assuming it is as good as it could be.

What to do next—Take a sober, systematic approach to greening your products:

- Get everyone on the same page. Common principles and a shared mental model help ensure that key questions get asked everywhere in the organization.

- Mix it up. Get design, logistics, and sourcing working together, so innovation isn't thwarted by decisions that were "already made" in some other silo.

- Start where you can. Your company doesn't control every process that contributes to its product, but you and your suppliers can learn from initial successes such as Wal-Mart, which convened suppliers and sustainable packaging experts to share best practices and create joint standards (see Truth 30, "Supply chain management and partnerships").

- Take it step by step. Green one product line first and then extend. Herman Miller started with a single line of Cradle-to-Cradle certified green chairs, which let it master the challenges in the process before rippling it out across the company.[3]

- Design with Nature. Guide your design with nature's laws in mind (see Truth 27, "Design with nature"). Make your products both efficient and out of materials nature can handle.[4]

- Consider EcoLabels and other third-party certifications for green products (see Truth 17, "Creating strong EcoLabels") that can guide you in green product design and communications.

- Be conservative, truthful, and transparent in your messaging and marketing (see Truth 16, "Green branding and messaging"). How can you prevent greenwashing? Say little; do much.

TRUTH

21

Product take-back

How many printer cartridges do you use a year? Where do they go when they're empty? Hewlett-Packard saw a way to reduce its use of new plastic resin by re-envisioning how it made its products. Their innovative plan to "close the loop" in cartridge production takes back used cartridges from consumers, and blends the plastic with recycled water bottles, to create a cartridge line with up to 75 percent recycled content.[1]

The results? Of course Hewlett-Packard's green printing innovations create less waste, but it also created savings for customers estimated at $2 million per year for the California state government alone. Do you think the reduction of materials cost has improved Hewlett-Packard's bottom line, too? Count on it.

From the waste stream to the production line—Product take-back occurs when a manufacturer takes responsibility for product or packaging material after the customer is done using it. The manufacturer reaps the benefits of material recovery, and the customer gets more convenient recycling—often at point of sale—instead of disposing of the used product. Beverage bottle recycling is the most familiar example (with a small deposit paid at point of purchase to provide incentive for closing the loop). Product take-back has been extended to tires and batteries in the United States and a growing number of consumer products in Europe—which is often the harbinger for future policies for the United States.

Patagonia's fleece take-back—Patagonia was an established green leader for its outdoor gear and clothing when it initiated its first product take-back program. Although it had cultivated a deep green brand, company leaders were troubled that its synthetic fleece garments would live for thousands years in landfills, so in 2005, it began product recycling by collecting worn-out fleece jackets to remanufacture into new fleece for new jackets.[2] The Common Threads Recycling Program installed collection stations in stores, started a mail-in program, and observed results so good that it now accepts other brands' Polartec garments into its recycling system. Patagonia needs less new material to make its products (a cost and energy savings), diverted waste from landfills (an environmental benefit), are planning for a complete closed-loop production system (a process improvement), and further built its brand.

Hewlett-Packard and e-waste—When the European Union implemented the Waste Electrical and Electronic Equipment Directive (WEEE Directive) in 2005, requiring producers to accept and properly recycle "end of life" equipment, Hewlett-Packard embraced the inevitable, investing in strategic product design. Rather than fighting the regulations, as some companies did, Hewlett-Packard saw the business benefits of leading its industry. Hewlett-Packard made "design for environment" a key part of its product design and business strategies. Hewlett-Packard formed a strategic alliance with mining giant Noranda to field an efficient—and profitable—take-back system that mines the exceptionally rich ores of modern society's high-tech detritus. Working technology is redeployed, and nonworking equipment is separated into its component plastics and metals—which are channeled into the recycled materials stream.

Reduce impact, increase value—Recovering material helps deliver more benefit with less material—what we've always described at Natural Logic as "More Value. Less Stuff."™ And because material flows embody a long chain of environmental consequences—including energy use and toxics disposal—reducing material flow is a key part of any strategy to reduce impacts.

There is a growing policy trend toward extended producer responsibility, such as the EU's WEEE Directive. Many U.S. cities and states have developed their own e-waste regulations.[3] This has provided entrepreneurial opportunities to independent recycling companies to process the equipment and divert electronics from the landfill.

Doing the right thing, made easy—There are multiple methods models of take-back (or "reverse logistics") programs; you can mix and match to best suit your company. What leads to a successful program? That differs by business and type of product.

- **In-store collection**—Patagonia takes back unwanted Polartec garments in its retail locations. This is also a shrewd marketing strategy because it gets customers back in the stores to look at new products. (On the other hand, it might generate extra car trips, which reduces the environmental benefit.)

- **Mail-in**—Hewlett-Packard's printer cartridge take-back saves the company the cost of new cartridge material because what the customer really wants is the ink. A postage-paid envelope packed in with new printer cartridges makes take-back an effortless and low-impact process.

- **Third-party collection and processing**—Best Buy and other retailers collect cell phones and batteries in bins at their stores, for processing by third-party companies that "mine" other companies' waste streams, "refine" the waste, and sell valuable materials back to original manufacturers.

Take-back strategies—Here are some take-back strategies you can use in your business:

- **Design for take-back**—Upstream planning and design are keys to any successful take-back program. Make products that are easily disassembled and use materials that are readily recyclable. Design what works before it's demanded by regulations.

- **Give the consumer options**—Make returns easier (in store and mail-in) to improve your rate of material recovery.

- **Reduce your own waste disposal costs by sourcing materials from vendors with a take-back system**—We've seen efforts as simple as use of reusable shipping pallets allowing companies to downsize their waste service (and save money on that as well).

- **Track your rate of successful take-backs**—For example, track the units recovered as a percentage of units sold. Then apply the same techniques you use in your production processes to adjust and optimize! Most companies are experts at finding out what makes customers buy but are just beginning to learn what works best in getting customers to play their part in product take-back schemes.

- **Go beyond "design for take-back"**—Adopt a "cradle-to-cradle" design strategy. Build closed loops into your logistics, sourcing, product design, and end-of-life recovery.

- **Consider selling services instead of products**—(See Truth 22, "Product to service.")

TRUTH

22

Product to service

Selling more product is the road to profit, right? Not always. IBM used to be in the business of selling big, expensive computers that only big businesses and governments could afford. The traditional model of invent, manufacture, and sell worked well enough, but IBM hit its stride when leadership realized what customers needed—customers didn't want powerful machines; they wanted powerful computing ability. On top of that, customers also had a demand for experts that could set up and customize the computers to their needs, so IBM launched its multimillion dollar "information solutions" service. IBM's customers now spend less time configuring their systems and have less downtime, so they can work more efficiently.

Hot showers, cold beer—Customers are interested in value and utility—the benefit they get from a product—not necessarily the material product itself. As Amory Lovins, Chairman and Chief Scientist at Rocky Mountain Institute, points out, "People don't want kilowatt-hours or lumps of coal or barrels of sticky black goo; they want hot showers and cold beer."[1] Many businesses are finding that moving from traditional product sales into delivering service (also known as servicizing[2]) can provide customers with more value and better quality, and generate higher returns. Product-to-service is not just rental; it's a business model and implementation strategy.

Companies in widely varied industries use the service model: Interface, Xerox, Apple's iTunes, Zip Car, Castrol, and Applied Materials, to name a few.

Service has its privileges—Servicizing (selling a service or function rather than a product) offers a number of potential business and environmental advantages:

- Servicizing requires less resource flow to satisfy a customer.
- A service builds ongoing relationships and repeat customers by embedding your business into customers' functions.
- Services can lower costs for your customers (both initial costs and total cost of ownership) and streamline the sales process for you.
- Servicizing can have environmental benefits by decreasing product throughput and "waste."

What kind of products work well as a service?—Good candidates for servicizing include the following:

- Products with long "post-use" lives (for example, carpet) or that require upgrades (for example, software)

- Toxics and products that are hard to dispose of (chemicals)

- Products with high initial costs (vehicles, manufacturing equipment, solar panels)

- Products that require technical knowledge to set up (computer networks)

Know where your service fits into the business ecosystem. Servicizing is familiar to some sectors (from automobile rental to office equipment leasing) but new to others, and pioneering can have its hiccups. Interface pioneered servicizing by leasing floor covering services in place of selling carpet tiles but struggled to close sales because its business customers were used to putting carpeting into the capital budget, not operating expenses.[3]

What you need to do—Be clear on what your customer actually wants from you and use your clear understanding of your customer's needs to guide thoughtful design. Design a business model that delivers your value with the least amount of material. Will you include a take-back program (see Truth 21, "Product take-back")? Will you incorporate maintenance and repairs in a higher price? There are many options and no single answer that works in all businesses.

- Identify the aspects of your business that could be servicized. Which products could be replaced by services? Which products could be complemented with added service?

- Start incrementally. Try turning one product into a service first to test the waters. You can learn valuable lessons that you can use if you decide to roll out a bigger service.

- Create the right messaging to sell your business' value as a service instead of just selling products. Tell and document stories that highlight added value; emphasize decreased downtime for customers, less time dealing with waste, lower cost-related risks, and the benefit to them of relying on your expertise.

TRUTH

23

What makes a service green?

Ray Anderson, founder and chairman of Interface, had a radical insight. He realized that people don't really want the carpeting Interface made. Instead, he concluded, they want floors that are attractive and comfortable to walk on. Anderson decided to lease floor covering services. Although carpet leasing was greener than carpet making—because it took a fraction as much energy and materials to satisfy a customer over time—how could Anderson ensure that his flooring service was as green as he envisioned?

Turning a product-and-material-based business into a service (see Truth 22, "Product to service") can reduce your environmental impact and increase profits. But that doesn't automatically make your service green. A truly green service must provide its value to its customers with the least amount of environmental impact. Just as with a green product, green services need to be resource-efficient, low on toxic materials, and as close to climate neutral as possible—not just in their creation but also in the purpose they serve to customers.

Why it's important—Servicizing can be a path to a greener business, but service businesses still consume material and energy resources, and not all services are equally green. Interface's service still requires production of carpeting, transportation, and energy for recycling. At thousands (or millions) of service customers per year, it adds up.

A truly green service must provide its value to its customers with the least amount of environmental impact.

Doing more with less—The intrinsic advantage of a green service is more efficient capital and resource utilization. Not everyone has to own things full time that they only use part time. You need to know how to identify and where to apply this service strategy—replacing what products, with what services, for which customers, meeting what needs—and when to sell a service instead of a product.

Interface, the commercial flooring company, backs up its Evergreen flooring lease by manufacturing the product in factories that have saved hundreds of millions of dollars by aggressively driving out energy and material waste. Interface installs and maintains the product (ensuring longer carpet life), in addition to replacing and recycling it when worn or out of favor. Interface even simplifies the purchase process for customers. With this model, everybody wins:

- Less waste
- Better profit margins
- "Stickier" customers for Interface
- Less hassle and better value for its customers
- Less flow of "stuff" from wellhead to landfill—about one-sixth for the same floor area

There's room for innovation, even in familiar product-to-service models. Zipcar, CityCarShare, now Hertz, and others[1] build on the car rental model (an early example of product to service) by providing convenient short-term rentals—a few hours instead of days. This enables customers to live without owning a car. ("Keeping a car in your driveway when you're concerned about global warming," Zipcar says, "is like keeping cookies in your cupboard when you're trying to lose weight.") And when they do drive, customers get fuel-efficient cars and pricing that encourages them to minimize their driving. Another multiple win: Customers save money, businesses make money, and environmental impact is reduced. (Unless, of course, convenient short-term rental services encourage more car use. No solution is without its problems and trade-offs, but that in turn just drives to the next solution—like offering more efficient vehicles in the short-term rental fleets, or pedal-powered vehicles, or even rethinking urban planning to require less transportation.)

What you need to do—As you think about how to make your services greener:

- Ask yourself and your customers, "What does the customer need, really?" What's the function that needs to be fulfilled? "If I want to hang a picture," Amory Lovins, Chairman and Chief Scientist at Rocky Mountain Institute, pithily observes, "I don't need a drill; I need a hole." Are you selling the solution best suited to your customers' real needs?

- Figure out how you can fulfill that need with service instead of product (see Truth 22). You're instantly greener because you need less stuff to produce the result. Then, determine how your service can be delivered as greenly as possible.

- Look at materials used in your service. Do you use high recycled content, recyclable, low carbon alternatives in your office supplies? If you're using or providing equipment, is it as energy-efficient as possible? Create an environmentally preferable purchasing plan (see Truth 29, "Environmentally preferable purchasing").

- Optimize your operations. Incorporate lean operating strategies (see Truth 13, "Running lean and green") into the delivery of your service. When you control your costs and continually improving your processes, you save money and resources, and that's a good thing.

- Localize and virtualize. Travel efficiently and try to reduce employee commute by using virtual meetings to replace air travel. Check out WebEx, GoToMeeting, Hewlett-Packard Virtual Meeting Room, Cisco TelePresence, or even Second Life (see Truth 39, "How IT can drive greening").

TRUTH

24

Biomimicry—learning
from life

When a Mercedes-Benz design team went to a local aquarium seeking inspiration from the sleek, fast-moving sharks, it found something shocking—a clumsy looking boxfish in another tank seemed to move with almost no drag and little effort. This discovery resulted in a boxfish-inspired design, wind tunnel tests, and finally a 70 mpg "Bionic" concept car with 80 percent lower nitrogen oxide emissions than the average car.[1]

As we at Natural Logic have long asked our clients, "Why reinvent the wheel, when nearly four billion years of R&D has already been done?"

Imitation of life in a good way—Biomimicry means "imitation of life." Author Janine M. Benyus calls biomimicry "doing it nature's way." She recommends looking to nature:

- **As model**—For inspiration, for design to solve human problems.

- **As mentor**—Focusing us on what we can learn from nature, rather than just extracting from it.

- **As measure**—Of what works, what's appropriate, and what lasts.

Changing the way we conduct business—Biomimicry, says Benyus (who coined the term), "has the potential to change the way we grow food, make materials, harness energy, heal ourselves, store information, and conduct business."

"Let's learn the basics from nature and build on that," she advises. "Waste is a resource, use energy wisely, use materials sparingly, take only what we need, diversify and cooperate, do what you know how to do."[2]

Naturally smarter design—Biomimicry considers three levels of design:

- Natural form (such as a fish-shaped car)
- Natural processes (such as green chemistry in creating the car)
- Ecosystems (such as industrial ecology—how the car impacts the world around it).

There are three approaches designers take to biomimicry: seeing nature as a model, mentor, and measure.[3]

- **Seeing nature as a model**—This is biomimicry on its most direct surface level. For example, designers might find an example in nature and use it as a model, as Pax Scientific (www.paxscientific.com) has done with fans and propellers modeled on whale fins and nautilus shells, or as Velcro famously did with fabric and other fasteners modeled on the hook-and-loop strategy of seed pods. This method uses nature's endlessly refined solutions to inspire innovation beyond conventional thinking.

- **Seeing nature as a mentor**—This approach mimics and adapts the principles and processes that nature uses in its creation of "products," learning from how nature makes trees, whales, and other "stuff." A forest ecosystem cycles nutrients through a complex set of plant and animal relationships that co-evolved to perform multiple, complex functions, powered by the sun and generating no waste. This approach evaluates how an industrial ecosystem can do the same.[4] (Think of it as a "model" at the scale of systems and principles.)

- **Seeing nature as measure**—Biomimicry sees nature as "a standard against which to judge the 'rightness' of our innovations. Are they life promoting? Do they fit in? Will they last?"[5] How do our products compare with such natural products as redwood trees, phytoplankton, aquifers, and ladybugs? How well will the manmade widgets integrate into the market and pre-existing natural product lines? Does the latest smart phone have the same staying power as a turtle, or will it go extinct—and turn to toxic waste—a year from now when the new model comes out? This element provides a constant refrain to the question of "How good is good enough?"

"We can begin to divine a canon of nature's laws," Benyus writes, echoing the design principles that have been identified by Hardin Tibbs, Bill McDonough, John Todd, myself, and others. "Nature runs on sunlight. Nature uses only the energy it needs. Nature fits form to function. Nature recycles everything. Nature rewards cooperation. Nature banks on diversity. Nature demands local expertise. Nature curbs excess from within. Nature taps the power of limits."

Although the principles appear to be universal, not all nature's designs work in every niche, so be diverse in your solutions. Think widely—make that wildly!—for materials and components. The lessons go on—integrative design, self-assembly, energy, material efficiency, and effectiveness.

One of the lessons of biomimicry is to optimize the performance of the entire system for the long term, rather than maximize the performance of parts of systems for the short term. (Maximize: Get the largest possible result for the selected system factor. Optimize: Get the best possible result for all relevant system factors.) This is as true of ecosystems as it is of production lines—as lean production systems have proven (see Truth 13, "Running lean and green").

Nature's next top model—The Speedo LZR Racer suit that Michael Phelps wore to win eight Olympic gold medals gained part of its magic from the study of preserved sharks.

Researchers learned that shark skin is covered in tiny "teeth" or dermal denticles. Their shape and positioning varies across the shark's body, managing the flow of water over the skin, reducing drag, and enabling the shark to "slide" through the sea with remarkable efficiency.[6]

Similarly, the U.S. Navy studied the structure and dynamics of dolphin skin to learn how to reduce drag on submarines.

Get inspired—Check out the work of some inspiring practitioners. The Biomimicry Institute (http://biomimicryinstitute.org) has developed an amazing database—www.asknature.org—providing systemic, searchable access to nature's treasure trove of design and a book summarizing "Nature's 100 Best"[7] innovations. And you don't have to be a designer or an engineer to get inspired.

TRUTH

25

Reducing your product footprints

A hiker leaves a footprint on a trail. What footprint does a cheeseburger leave? Futurist Jamais Cascio has calculated that the carbon footprint (see Truth 14, "Carbon footprinting") of the cheeseburgers consumed in the United States per year works out to 195,750,000 metric tons of CO_2 equivalent—equal to the carbon emissions of 19.6 million Hummer H3 SUVs![1] Give or take a million.

But footprinting is not just about carbon.

What's a footprint?—Raw materials, the transportation, the land used, and the energy to render the product all leave their impact in the environment. A "footprint" is a measurement of the life cycle impact on resources (such as energy, water, and "waste," as well as carbon). A footprint also is the measurement of systems (such as the productive capacity of arable land) generated in the production and use of a given item. Footprinting can be used on large systems (national water use or corporate carbon emissions) or for individual products, such as that cheeseburger. And it can be used for specific resources, such as carbon or water footprints, or to gauge more holistic impacts, such as an ecological footprint.

Ecological footprints—An *ecological* footprint is a measure of how much biologically productive land and water (of earth's finite surface area) is used or impacted by a product's manufacture, use, and "disposal," and the assimilation of its "wastes." (We put "disposal" in quotes for the same reason we use quotes for "waste" as a reminder that there is no "away," and that there's no such thing as "waste" [see Truth 11, "Waste? Not! Eliminating non-product"].) Think of it as a budgeting tool for reality-based accounting (see Truth 46, "Reality-based accounting").

The ecological footprint has thus far been used more to calculate the resource consumption of nations and the world as a whole rather than the resource impact of products; the United States, for example, operates at an ecological deficit with a footprint 50 percent to 100 percent larger that its biocapacity, whereas Canada's biocapacity is more that 150 percent larger than its footprint. It's still challenging to break down the data meaningfully for companies and products but should get easier as tools and data improve.

The ecological footprint is usually measured in global hectares (hectares with world-average productivity).[2] Earth's current ecological footprint is about 1.3 planets.[3] Projections show that if we continue at our current rate, we will require the resources of two planets by the early 2030s.[4] Houston, we've got a budget problem!

Earth's ecological footprint is about 1.3 planets. We'll require the resources of two planets by the early 2030s. Houston, we've got a budget problem!

How big is your foot?—Tracking footprints helps you know where you stand in relation to your competitors, or to policy goals, or to your own goals. Tracking also helps you decide where to focus your efforts to reduce that footprint. Before New Belgium Brewing Co. developed a carbon footprint of a six-pack of its Fat Tire Amber Ale in 2007, the company assumed transportation and shipping had the biggest impact and was, therefore, the best target for reducing carbon emissions. The analysis delivered surprising and strategically significant results. Transportation came in unexpectedly low at fourth place—after glass bottle manufacturing, growing hops and barley, and refrigeration.[5]

Now New Belgium is focusing on using higher recycled content in its bottles and is considering using organic—and less carbon-intensive—ingredients and is jumping ahead of both competitors and emerging carbon regulations.

It's in there—Embodied energy—a measure of the energy used over a product's entire life cycle to manufacture, transport, use, and dispose of the product—can be a valuable tool for assessing the ROI of energy-efficiency strategies and new energy technologies.[6] Energy footprints contribute to the analysis of carbon footprints and also provide a valuable check on the *energy* ROI of alternative energy investments.[7]

A product's carbon footprint is determined much the same way as a company's:

1. Determine all emission sources up and down the supply chain.

2. Make an explicit decision of how much of the supply chain to include.

3. Gather data.

4. Apply emissions factors.

5. Review and share the results.

6. Document your assumptions!

To determine an *ecological* footprint, you need to determine the demand, typically measured in global hectares, that your product (or more likely, company) places on earth's biocapacity and compare that with the "budgeted" biocapacity allocated on a land area, or revenue population basis.[8]

What you need to do

- Track your footprints—whether carbon, water, or ecological—over time so you know if you're improving. NGOs such as Global Footprint Network (www.GlobalFootprint.org) can provide do-it-yourself footprint calculators to help you measure your footprint or point you to specialists who can.

- Estimate the footprint of a product you sell (or buy). What could you do to decrease its footprint? What would it take to reduce it to zero?

- Communicate product footprints to your customers—and your designers and buyers to help them make more informed choices, as companies from Wal-Mart and Tesco to Bon Appétit and New Belgium Brewing Co. are beginning to do.

- Consider whether product footprints and company footprints should be a factor in your purchasing criteria, both to support your green branding and to reduce your future risk (see Truth 45, "Profit, value, and risk").

TRUTH

Cradle to cradle

The term cradle to cradle (coined by Walter R. Stahel in 1970 and popularized by William McDonough and Michael Braungart in their 2002 book of that name) refers to design processes that see materials as perpetually circulated in safe, healthy, closed-loop metabolisms.[1] This is contrasted to traditional cradle-to-grave products, which are released into the environment or dumped in landfills at the end of their "life."

Are you finished with that?—We moderns think of products in a "Take/Make/Waste" framework: We take the raw materials from the environment, we make a product, and when we're done with it, we throw it "away," with little regard for its impacts.

The Cradle-to-Cradle (C2C) framework expands that view to include the product's life cycle, from initial resource extraction through the end of its life, while considering the biological impacts of its cyclicity and toxicity.

The C2C framework recognizes two distinct "metabolisms" within which materials flow. Distinguishing between biological and technical nutrients and managing materials in closed loops maximize and enhance material value without damaging life support systems.

- Biological nutrients are safely consumable or biodegradable by living systems (or otherwise naturally degradable)—materials posing no immediate or eventual hazard to living systems—that can be used for human purposes and be safely returned to the environment to feed ecological processes. Products made from biological nutrients are also called "products of consumption" because they are designed for safe and complete return to the environment to become nutrients for healthy living systems. Examples include food, wood, and cotton.

- Technical nutrients are not safely consumable by living systems. Technical nutrients are materials, frequently synthetic or mineral, that need to remain in a closed-loop system of manufacture, recovery, and reuse (the technical metabolism), maintaining its highest value through many product life cycles. Technical nutrients are used in "products of service," which are durable goods that render a service to customers. The C2C system proposes that products of service be used by the customer but

owned by the manufacturer—
either formally or in effect—to the
benefit of both. The manufacturer
maintains ownership of
valuable material assets for
continual reuse—and a long-
term relationship with returning
customers—while customers
receive the service of the product

Nature didn't evolve by wasting material, or accumulating toxic materials. Why should you?

without assuming its material liability (an "eco-lease" [see Truth
22, "Product to service"]). The environment benefits, too, because
the closed technical nutrient cycle minimizes toxic impacts,
and the product of service strategy uses less resource to meet
human needs. Examples include metals and persistent synthetic
chemicals.

Know your nutrients—Thinking "cradle to cradle" means getting
familiar with the stuff of your stuff—the materials that make up
the things you make and use, and where they fit in C2C's two
metabolisms:

- Understand the material cycles of the industrial ecosystem.
  Nature didn't evolve by wasting material, or accumulating toxic
  materials. Why should you? (See Truth 24, "Biomimicry—learning
  from life.")

- Eliminate toxic materials, or manage them in closed "technical
  nutrient cycles." Zeftron Nylon and the lead in automobile
  batteries are examples of technical nutrients, ideally circulating
  in closed loops with the material—at least in theory—always
  remetabolized somewhere.[2]

Be efficient. Do more with less. But don't stop there. Make products
that are eco-effective, not just eco-efficient. "What's the point," Bill
McDonough asks, "of doing the wrong thing more efficiently?" Why
just reduce the damage when you could potentially eliminate it?
Why just eliminate the bad stuff when you could design restorative
products? Eco-effective means safe, profitable, and regenerative
products that produce economic, ecological, and social value.[3] (See
Truth 10, "Eco-efficiency: Good for business and the environment.")

Is recycling a cradle-to-cradle process? Not necessarily. Recycling "downcycles"[4] materials into lower-quality uses. For example, when you recycle a plastic bottle, the material loses functionality and value—it typically becomes a park bench, not another bottle. Recycling beats landfill, but ecological and economic benefits are greater if a bottle returns as a bottle—or is even "upcycled" into something of greater value, like clothing.

Keep your value out of the trash—It's time to design solutions upstream rather than manage problems downstream.

- Rethink your design. Think first about the value your product gives your customers, *then* about the materials needed.

- Inventory the materials that make up your product and identify which ones can be replaced by something that could provide the same (or better) value. For example, replace technical nutrients with biological. Replace hazardous technical nutrients with less hazardous ones, or replace technical nutrients likely to disperse with ones likely to be cycled effectively.

- Make your product with materials recoverable to your own company, to other firms, or to worms in a compost bin. Just make it edible to *someone*.

- Stop designing "waste" into your production process (or assuming it has to be there). Challenge your designers to create products so that all materials are recovered.

- Keep technical nutrients out of biological cycles. McDonough describes a chair upholstered with a weave of "recyclable" polypropylene and "compostable" cotton—a blend that thwarts both plastics recycling (the plastic doesn't decompose in a landfill and doesn't return to the technical cycle) and good composting. Using materials that are durable and can also be safely absorbed by the nitrogen cycle, such as upholstery fabric Climatex Lifecycle, ensures that the textile's nutrients can be returned into nature's biological metabolism.[5]

- Consider getting your product formally certified to the Cradle-to-Cradle standard.[6]

TRUTH

Design with nature

"Our eyes do not divide us from the world, but unite us with it. Let this be known to be true. Let us then abandon the simplicity of separation and give unity its due. Let us abandon the self-mutilation which has been our way and give expression to the potential harmony of man-nature. The world is abundant, we require only a deference born of understanding to fulfill man's promise. Man is that uniquely conscious creature who can perceive and express. He must become the steward of the biosphere. To do this he must design with nature."—Ian McHarg[1]

The term *Design with Nature* was popularized by urban planner and landscape architect Ian McHarg in his 1969 book of the same name. He wrote about the need to consider the unique qualities, functions, and ambient resources of a place and translate them into planning and designing buildings, neighborhoods, and cities in harmony with nature. Although the book focused on the local environment's influence on place-based planning and architecture (and pioneered the use of overlay maps to resolve competing ideas about land use), its many lessons are far-reaching and applicable to business today. Two key lessons: Adapt to the place you're in, whether watershed or planet, and use what's there wisely and elegantly, without damaging that place.

Looking at the land use example more globally, it means using models found in nature to design products, processes, and businesses. It provides businesses with a framework for strategy, innovation, and success (see Truth 24, "Biomimicry—learning from life").

The well-being of our economy fundamentally depends on the ecological services that support it. Design with nature is the key to achieving business goals while maintaining or enhancing nature's services.[2]

Designs that consider—and emulate—nature are more likely to succeed. They surf natural resource flows rather than fight them (think naturally air-conditioned adobe houses in desert climes). They use design principles tested and refined in evolutionary time. They use materials that renew, replenish, and support life's cycles.

And designing with nature, like any well-chosen constraint, can drive innovation (see Truth 28, "Innovation is at the heart of greening").

Designing with nature—Designing with nature has a simple metabolic basis. Industrial systems can use only two things—energy and materials—and they release only product and non-product. (Although living systems, of course, produce no non-product at all.) Good design should mirror nature's processes, meaning that they should minimize material and energy inputs, minimize use (and eliminate release) of toxic substances, maximize product value, eliminate non-product, and rely on renewable energies to drive the process.

■ Understand that living systems run on renewable energy and closed loops of edible materials (the "waste" of one is food for another).

■ Take stock of ambient resources and use the ones that are locally abundant. For example, when we helped a client plan a new resort, we designed around the ambient flows of the place—landscaping that can survive on local rainfall alone and buildings designed (in orientation, efficiency, and technology) to use ambient solar and wind energy for heating, cooling, and electricity generation. These flows aren't just resources you can take from, but natural systems you can enhance as well.

Nature utilizes a free and abundant supply and doesn't overshoot that supply.

■ Design with renewable materials and renewable energy, as nature does. Almost all living systems depend on photosynthesis to capture current solar income. Nature utilizes a free and abundant supply and doesn't overshoot that supply.

■ Design waste out of your system. Use less material by designing long-lasting products and dematerializing where possible (see Truth 22, "Product to service"). Design for long-term optimization, rather than short-term maximization. Use reusable, renewable, recyclable, and "pre-owned" materials.

■ Close and shorten material loops. Make products that are "edible," using materials that can be used by other businesses or absorbed in nature without damage.

Don't assume a necessary tradeoff between design with nature and design for profit. Insist on both.

■ Don't sell, make—or buy—what can't be metabolized by living systems. If you do create toxins, synthesize them as needed, rather than stockpiling them. (You don't see a rattlesnake hauling around tankers full of venom, do you?)

■ Design diverse products and systems with a rich variety of interconnections of function and resource exchange.

■ Be profitable. A tree uses solar energy to grow its "profit"—the creation of seeds and, eventually, new trees (and more than 50 other benefits to its surrounding ecosystem). If your business isn't profitable, it won't be around long enough to create "seeds" of economic well-being or create designs that benefit nature. Here's the key: Don't assume a necessary trade-off between design with nature and design for profit. Insist on both.

TRUTH

28

Innovation is at the heart of greening

"If you are in a shipwreck and all the lifeboats are gone, a piano top...that comes along makes a fortuitous life preserver, but this is not to say that the best way to design a life preserver is in the form of a piano top. I think that we are clinging to a great many piano tops in accepting yesterday's fortuitous contrivings."—Buckminster Fuller

Innovation is intrinsic to the human experience, and certainly at the heart of our modern, interconnected, 24/7 global society. Our lives are transformed and our economies powered by innovation that meets unmet needs and builds new value (and sometimes creates new problems along the way).

Innovation is also at the heart of greening, whether you see it as building a better mousetrap or driving a new industrial revolution. My vote: Both! Greening products, businesses, and entire economies is about innovation. Whether innovation looks like stunning breakthroughs or modest, incremental improvements, like leaps of genius or "slow and steady wins the race," the first step is unlocking the tyranny of "we've always done it this way."

The ways we've always done it were often the innovations of their own times—the age of cheap energy, endless frontiers, unpriced externalities (see Truth 46, "Reality-based accounting"), and growth at all costs. We're in a new world—carbon-constrained, "hot, flat, and crowded,"[1] with many chickens coming home to roost—that will reward innovation suited to this emerging reality.

> ...the first step is unlocking the tyranny of "we've always done it this way."

"Innovation," says Harvard professor Michael Porter, "is the central issue in economic prosperity."

What you need to know—Innovation might seem to be a random and fortuitous process, but people, companies, and nations have gotten consistently good at it (think Leonardo Da Vinci, Thomas Edison, Bell Labs, Japan, and Silicon Valley).

How do you move it from random to systematic and reliable? In the 1960s, NASA's "Department of It Can't Be Done" transformed "impossible" performance requirements into design specifications that could be systematically rendered to practice—more than 3,000 times in the course of the Apollo program.

Your business might not seem like a moon mission, but if you have goals that might seem beyond reach, or at least beyond current resources or know how—and you should (see Truth 7, "How green is good enough?," and Truth 52, "Future proofing")—then part of your job is inventing your future, even if your business is only about flipping burgers. (Look at what Ray Kroc did with McDonalds.)

Where do you look for innovation? Management guru Peter Drucker wrote of "seven sources of innovation":

- Unexpected occurrences
- Perception-reality incongruities
- Process weakness or needs
- Industry and market changes
- Demographic changes
- Changes in buyer attitudes and priorities
- New scientific and business knowledge

I suggest an eighth: looking to nature for design inspiration, and as a model for how to design (see Truth 24, "Biomimicry—learning from life").

What you need to do—There's no cookbook for innovation, but here are some ideas to help make innovation an intrinsic part of your business:

- Invite it, support it, and systematize it (but not so much that systems squash spontaneity).
- Build what Peter Senge calls a "learning organization" (one that develops shared and individual learning to continually enhance its ability to adapt).
- Go sideways. Or backward. Or inside out. Or upside down.[2] New perspectives make new thoughts possible.
- Bring together diverse design teams—people from inside and outside your company—who not only have a stake in the outcome, but also are likely to have substantially different insights about what's needed and how to get there.

Keep the process open, focusing on "how we can" rather than "why we can't."

- Be clear, and complete, about the design criteria that will satisfy your goals.

- Insist, tenaciously, on meeting them all, without compromise. (Yes, eventually you'll probably have to accept some trade-offs. Resist it as long as you can. Start the no-compromise process over again with the next generation of goals.)

- Make "design" the fundamental conversation in your organization. Visionary architect and inventor Buckminster Fuller's basic protocol in his World Game workshops—where I got my basic training—was straightforward and effective:

  - Define the present state of affairs.

  - Define the preferred state (as specifically as possible).

  - Explore pathways that connect the two, scanning backward from the success, as well as forward from the problem.

  - Keep the process open, focusing on "how we can" rather than "why we can't."

Don't let fear of failure keep you from experimenting—and don't let success breed complacency. The business world is littered with once-successful companies that stopped innovating because what they were doing worked well. Compare Toyota and GM. It's clear which one has built innovation into its core practices.

The business world is littered with once-successful companies that stopped innovating because what they were doing worked well.

It's a familiar story: A respected leader—a business executive, a politician, a scientist—says something can't be done, or is a bad idea, or is too expensive. Then an arrogant upstart comes along with a modest innovation, or sometimes a world-changing one. The innovation might be met first with dismissal— "it's impossible"—then with enthusiasm, and finally with "oh, that's not so innovative; everyone knows that."

TRUTH

Environmentally preferable purchasing

You purchase supplies or order equipment. You're spending money and using resources. Where are they made? Do they support jobs, businesses, and the tax base in your region? In the United States? In other countries? Does their production create unnecessary pollution? Are they recyclable? Are they made of recycled materials? What impact does this have on your people? What will the supplies or equipment cost to operate—in both money and energy over their lifetimes? What "wastes" are created by your purchasing decisions? How will you dispose of them?

Big customers—from the U.S. government to Wal-Mart—are increasingly incorporating these questions into their purchasing specifications, and using Environmentally Preferable Purchasing (EPP) to specify procurement of products and services that are less harmful to the environment and workers in comparison to other products.

The responsibility of choice—Every purchase your company makes is a vote. Every time you drop a dollar, yen, yuan, euro, rial, or pound on the shop counter or write a corporate procurement order, you're voting to support a type of product, service, or business, and to set in motion a stream of consequences, in your business and in the world.

EPP is powerful because organized purchasing power of large corporate and institutional buyers—including state and local government in the United States—can stimulate the market for green goods. The U.S. government's decision to require LEED certified buildings (see Truth 33, "LEED standards for green buildings") was a significant driver of the green building industry. The "license to operate" in the European Union is increasingly dependent on a company's ability to deliver environmentally preferable products.

Your business customers, too, are increasingly looking at environmental attributes when considering your products and services. When Wal-Mart decided to source organic cotton for its yoga outfits, the impact was so large that it made the organic cotton source viable for other customers, such as Patagonia. And Wal-Mart's EPP directives to its 60,000 suppliers are having more impact in changing the face of U.S. business than any boatload of EPA regulations ever did.

Planet or plastic?—When considering EPP, here are some things you should take into consideration:

- Be clear what's important to your customers—and their customers.

- Browse some other companies' EPP guidelines on the web to get ideas.

- Include key environmental criteria in your purchasing specifications. Review your company's purchasing invoices (or even the supply closet) and check your inventory against some environmental scorecards; borrow one from your key customers, your industry association, EPA, or the big dogs at Wal-Mart. After you identify items that should be replaced, see if your suppliers have alternatives available to meet your requirements, or if they can develop them.

- Use life-cycle thinking. You're not going to conduct a life-cycle analysis for every purchase, or every time you shop. "Paper or plastic?" is complicated enough. But you can apply life-cycle thinking (see Truth 20, "What makes a product green?") to your design, purchasing, and operations decisions. For example, when you purchase a printer, you can consider its energy efficiency, ink yields, duplexing capacity, and both cartridge and end-of-life recycling options.

- Don't buy things you don't need or too much of what you do need, and don't buy goods that come with packaging you don't need since you get stuck with the disposal bill.

> Don't buy things you don't need, too much of what you need, or goods that come with packaging you don't need.

- Create a company EPP policy. Typical policies list waste minimization, recycled content, energy efficiency, pollution, and toxicity as criteria for purchasing. You can develop your own criteria and priority or look to an external source such as the U.S. EPA[1] for guidance. The EPA even has tools to help you calculate the potential benefits from environmentally preferable purchasing.

- Make sure the goods you sell are environmentally preferable, too, or you could miss out on major government contracts (and, increasingly, corporate procurement, too). Check the criteria listed by governments and industry groups to see if your products make the grade and reengineer products that don't. The U.S. government only purchases goods defined by Executive Order 13423.[2] States and many cities have their own EPP guidelines.

- Look for opportunities to get your product or business green-certified, so your customers instantly know what they're getting (see Truth 17, "Creating strong EcoLabels").

Enlightened self-interest—For whatever you buy, there is most likely a guide to finding preferable products. Here are a few places where you can find EPP guidelines:

- U.S. Environmental Protection Agency—www.epa.gov

- Stop Waste—www.stopwaste.org

- Green Seal—www.greenseal.org

...altruism is self-interest. It just depends where you draw the boundaries of "self."

EPP isn't altruism. The practices of every member of the global supply chain that each of your purchases activates affect both quality of life and economic viability—both of which affect you. As a wise person once said, in the big picture, altruism is self-interest.[3] (It just depends where you draw the boundaries of "self.")

TRUTH

Supply chain management and partnerships

What you buy determines what you make into product and what you create as non-product (see Truth 11, "Waste? Not! Eliminating non-product"). Environmentally preferable purchasing is one way to control this issue, as described in Truth 29, "Environmentally preferable purchasing." But what do you do if what you require needs to change, or if what your supplier sells is no longer what you need? You can shop around for new suppliers, or if you're big enough (like Wal-Mart), you can demand that your suppliers change what they offer. In most cases, you're somewhere in between. If you're smart enough, you can engage and influence your supplier—so you buy only what you want.

Partnerships are a powerful way to green your supply chain because they help you build a network of trusted suppliers to work collaboratively across an industry. By sharing information and meeting each other's needs, you can make supply-chain partnerships profitable and innovative while increasing the quality of your products.

If you're smart enough, you can engage and influence your supplier....

"There's a powerful synergy emerging," says Eric Olson of Business for Social Responsibility. "While more companies are making environmental performance demands of their supply chain, very few have yet figured out how to do that in a way that makes money for all partners. In fact, the environmental drivers are not a cost, but can be a key to discovering new business opportunities."[1]

Here's what you need to know about supply-chain management:

- Know the drivers of green supply chain efforts. When the WEEE Directive (see Truth 8, "Green regulations") was introduced in the EU, computing giants Hewlett-Packard, Dell, and IBM jointly issued a suppliers' code of conduct[2] as a response. This code of conduct helped consolidate and standardize "compliance, audit, and reporting efforts, [so] suppliers can focus on achieving the high standards of performance set forth by the code."

- Know what you need from your suppliers to create the service, product, and non-product output streams your business wants

...you can make supply-chain partnerships profitable and innovative while increasing the quality of your products.

to produce. Know what your suppliers need from you to provide what you need. (There's no magic bullet here; sit down with key suppliers, share current needs and future concerns, and figure out what to do about it. Working collaboratively can help create a network of trusted suppliers across an industry.)

■ Know the Toyota Production System, and how its systems of feedback and signals can help optimize relationships with your external suppliers and customers (see Truth 13, "Running lean and green").

■ Get clear on what matters to you. One place to start: Use a simple map of your key material flows, and your supply chain to determine your most significant non-products (in terms of amounts, cost, and environmental impact), and which suppliers are the most significant contributors.

■ Use an integrated design process. Design your supply chain as you design your product. This can help you select components and materials that optimize your supply chain's environmental performance.

■ Ask your suppliers to use sustainable materials and practices. Wal-Mart is getting its suppliers to use sustainable packaging because it's big and has influence, but also because it provides assistance. The New United Motor Manufacturing, Inc. (NUMMI) in Fremont, CA, reduced cardboard consumption by 60 percent by requiring suppliers to use reusable shipping containers, saving the company millions of dollars. NUMMI even returns protective plastic packaging to suppliers for reuse, resulting in additional annual savings of $99,000.[3]

■ Collaborate. Wal-Mart has convened 13 sustainable value networks[4] including Wal-Mart, suppliers, NGOs, academia, and consultants to develop standards, goals, and scorecards, and to share knowledge.

TRUTH

Supplier scorecards

In November 2006, Wal-Mart announced that it would initiate a sustainable packaging scorecard for all of its suppliers; the message was "score high on the green categories, or you're off the list." Wal-Mart gave suppliers a year to figure out how to comply and test strategies to reduce the amount of packaging used for products shipped to the retailer. A few weeks later, it hosted a suppliers summit to facilitate partnerships and help its suppliers learn how to meet their carbon reduction, cube utilization (a measure of storage efficiency in warehousing and shipping containers), material value, and other goals.[1]

As of November 2008, Wal-Mart's Sam's Club division had 90 percent participation from its suppliers, and Wal-Mart had a total of 250,000 product items entered into the scorecard.[2]

Because of Wal-Mart's giant scale, the potential environmental benefits of its corporate reduction goal could be staggering. Supplier scorecards are one of its key tools.

Roadmap for increasing value—Companies often use scorecards to provide a consistent and systematic way to communicate their needs to their supply chain, and to rate suppliers on quality, price, delivery time, customer service, and increasingly, environmental performance. Scorecards help embed a system of best practices into everyday decisions. Green scorecards also give buyers and supply chain managers a roadmap for incorporating green into their sourcing decisions.

This can save you money. For example, using scorecards that ensure your managers always consider energy efficiency in purchasing will save you money on operating expenses.

If you're a supplier, knowing you're going to be ranked on your environmental performance can be strong impetus to improve your own environmental performance—both to protect customer relations and reap your own efficiency benefits.

Get to know your unknown unknowns—What's driving this move to scorecards? Supplier scorecards have become an important communication tool as regulations and trade partnerships grow. Growing consumer demand for greener products also drives the use of scorecards (see Truth 30, "Supply chain management and partnerships"). The market is demanding more transparency, and companies need to manage exposure. In a conversation with Wal-Mart senior sustainability director Rand Waddoups, Whole Foods regional president Michael Bensacon observed, "The more questions you ask, the more answers you get that you don't want to hear."[3]

...you're asking for a regulator—or some blogger—to bust you for what you should have already controlled.

But better for you to hear it first. Whether you want to hear the truth about your supply chain, knowing the challenges your suppliers face in meeting your goals allows you to act to improve their performance. Otherwise, you're asking for a regulator—or some blogger—to bust you for what you should have already controlled.

What you need to do—This is another area where a systematic approach can reap business and environmental benefits:

- Create a system for ranking your suppliers—or add key environmental performance criteria to your existing systems for choosing suppliers (see Truth 29, "Environmentally preferable purchasing").

- Include key stakeholders in developing those criteria. Wal-Mart's packaging scorecard system was developed in cooperation with the trade group Packaging Sustainable Value Network and included important criteria such as CO_2 per ton of production, recycled content, and innovation. During the one-year trial period, suppliers gave input on what metrics were working and what needed adjustment.

- Embed scorecards in your practices at all levels, so employees learn to look for environmental data on supplier scorecards. Swedish construction and property management company JM Bygg began a program in the 1990s to fight "sick building syndrome." In addition to bad PR, it was losing millions in repair costs and lost hours from sick workers. Bygg developed a ranked database of acceptable construction products (low toxicity, high recycled content, natural materials) that it used in procurement and contractor education programs—and rewarded its buyers

Know what your customers are looking for and what their standards are. The easiest way to find out? Ask!

for buying green without hurting budgets, schedules, or quality. Bygg also provided this information to the building owners, as an ingredient list. By controlling its supply chain, it built a powerful environmentally friendly brand that, among other things, speeded its permitting process and increased trust in the communities it works in.[4]

- Use the scorecards to communicate your expectations to your suppliers. This can influence their practices, and you can work together for mutual benefit.

- Perform well as a supplier. Know what your customers are looking for and what their standards are. The easiest way to find out? Ask!

- Engaging your supply chain partners in dialogue is a great way to start finding win-win solutions. Share your own experience with them to help them develop scorecards and ensure that you appear in their system as a high scorer.

What next?

- Research the Wal-Mart packaging reduction initiative.

- Get clear on your key environmental concerns (see Truth 7, "How green is good enough," and Truth 42, "Keeping score").

- Communicate to suppliers—and buyers.

- Keep score. Incorporate your green scorecards into your regular performance review.

TRUTH

32

Clearing the rising bar

Environmental regulations have gotten ever more stringent, and we expect the bar to continue rising worldwide. (As I write this, automobile efficiency standards in China—long considered a laggard in environmental regulation—have leapfrogged those in the United States.) If you believe the myth that environmental compliance has to cost you money, you'll resist regulation and delay compliance as long as possible. If you recognize the potential profit opportunity in environmental improvement, you'll create a system for staying ahead of continually rising standards—eliminating waste, improving quality, and increasing value along the way.

Staying above the rising bar makes good business sense and not only because it can be profitable. If you're constantly reacting, you risk losing market share to innovators, while you're spending more time and resources adjusting. Being reactive is no way to run a successful business. Besides, playing catch-up is no way to live.

Understand what's driving the rising bar, and you'll have a better chance of "skating to where the puck is going to be."[1] I see three main drivers:

- Consumers demanding better environmental performance.

- Governments looking for ways to limit environment damage—and to guide investment toward the environmental and economic benefits of the "new energy economy."

> Being reactive is no way to run a successful business. Besides, playing catch-up is no way to live.

- Businesses looking to reduce risk and build profits, and for greener suppliers to support greener products and operations.

Underlying all these: Humans coming to terms with the inescapable physical realities that underlie our economic well-being (see Truth 9, "Secrets hiding in plain sight").

How to stay above the rising bar

- Guide your actions by physical reality, not regulatory thresholds (see Truth 8, "Green regulations"). Nature has evolved systems that run on renewable energy, with closed material loops, and only temporary and limited use of toxic materials. Human society—through both regulations and markets—is gradually moving in that direction. Your business can wait to be dragged, kicking and screaming, into that future—or it can lead the way. An example:

> Your business can wait to be dragged, kicking and screaming, into that future—or it can lead the way.

A tech client called us in to help craft a letter, requested by its largest customer, providing assurance that it would eliminate certain restricted substances by the end of the year. We declined—and upped the ante. "You don't need a letter," we said. "You need a letter *and* a design strategy that will get you out in front of the tougher request that you'll definitely get next year, and again the year after that."

- Pay attention to "the man behind the curtain"—the principles (not always obvious, but evident if you know where to look) driving the regulatory and market changes (see Truth 9). When the European Union activated its electronics take-back directive in 2005, nearly half of the global electronics industry were unprepared, with one-third of global revenues at risk. But half were prepared, and some, such as Hewlett-Packard, built new businesses to profit from the "surprise" that they saw coming. The key to hitting a moving target is to have systems that help you continually adjust your aim and build your organization's understanding of the new trends and patterns to be watching for and new questions to be asking, from the corporate suite to the loading dock.

- Build continuous improvement into your management systems with lean and green methods (see Truth 13, "Running lean and green"). Keep an active scan of market leaders. Use active feedback loops and clear communication to create a culture of continuous improvement that thrives on clearing the rising bar.

- Run an efficient business. Minimizing waste in your processes and materials makes it easier to adjust your course and adapt quickly.

- Measure and track your performance. The best way to set your course through the regulatory minefield is to know where you stand, and where you're heading (see Truth 42, "Keeping score"). You can help keep the process on track by providing relevant feedback throughout your organization and your supply chain.

- Ask "What if?" What if regulations become unexpectedly more demanding? What if prices of key resources change suddenly? What if a competitor delivers leapfrog innovation? What if the market falls out from under you? (See Truth 51, "Scenario planning.")

- Don't assume anything. Encourage your teams to regularly shift their point of view. Instead of "How much will this hurt?" and "How can we postpone dealing with it?" ask "What opportunity does this open for us?" and "How could meeting this need or demand benefit us, improve quality, and grow profit?"

- But most of all, play to the natural logic—those inescapable physical realities and laws of nature that underlie our economic well-being (see Truth 9). There's a reason we chose Natural Logic as the name of my company, folks.

TRUTH

33

LEED standards for green buildings

Buildings account for nearly half of all greenhouse gas emissions in the United States. Almost all our businesses operate in buildings. So green buildings can play an enormous part in bringing emissions down, or driving them further up. The decisions we make with regard to green buildings are made all the more significant because building design and construction decisions have impacts that last decades.

LEED (Leadership in Energy and Environmental Design) is the most widely used U.S. standard for certifying green buildings. The rating system provides guidelines related to design, construction, and operation of buildings. When a building is LEED-certified, it is designated as "Certified," "Silver," "Gold," or "Platinum" status, reflecting increasingly higher standards of green building. The U.S. Green Building Council, a Washington, DC-based nonprofit, created the rating system in 1998, and accredited third-party groups have since certified thousands of buildings in the United States and abroad.

Standards drive the green building market—Standards are powerful in green building; they provide a frame of reference, a basic how-to, and a tool for driving market demand that has transformed the building and development landscape in the United States in less than a decade. Because LEED has emerged as the preeminent (though not the only) rating system for green buildings, if you're interested in building a new green building or retrofitting an existing building, you need to know about LEED.

> Many cities around the country are adopting policies that require new buildings to be built to the LEED standard.

Many cities around the country are adopting policies that require new buildings to be built to the LEED standard. Atlanta, Dallas, and Los Angeles have already introduced LEED requirements into building codes for city-run facilities, though these regulations vary in scope. Los Angeles expedites permitting for projects that pursue LEED Silver certification or higher—saving builders from one to six months in the process. Dallas requires city-owned buildings larger than 10,000 square feet to be built to a LEED Silver standard.[1] It also plans to roll out similar requirements for commercial buildings and homes in the near future.

Green building is an important step toward addressing the enormous impact that buildings have on the environment. Having a standard in place helps designers and builders learn the green building process and communicate about their green efforts.

LEED rating systems—There are different LEED Rating Systems for different building types, including: LEED for New Construction (NC), LEED for Existing Building (EB), LEED for Schools, LEED for Homes, LEED for Retail, LEED for Commercial Interiors, LEED for Healthcare, and LEED for Core and Shell.

The LEED Rating System is organized in six sections, with points assigned for individual measures in each section:

- Sustainable sites (addressing land use)
- Water efficiency
- Energy and atmosphere
- Materials and resources
- Indoor environmental quality
- Innovation and design process

LEED certification is based on a point system—the number of points earned qualifies the building for different levels of LEED certification. The point system allows for some design flexibility because each section presents multiple opportunities to earn points.

LEED Certified	26–32 points
LEED Silver	33–38 points
LEED Gold	39–51 points
LEED Platinum	52–69 points

Construction of LEED buildings doesn't have to cost any more than regular buildings (see Truth 34, "The cost of building green"), although there are staffing costs associated with the actual documentation and certification process. Those costs are highly variable and depend on the size and number of buildings on a site, whether each building is new or renovated, and whether individual buildings or the entire site is being certified. These costs appear to be coming down over time, as practitioners gain experience and develop systems to streamline the process.

LEEDing the way

- Hire LEED Accredited Professionals to design, build, or renovate your building. Architecture firms, engineering firms, and construction companies are likely to have accredited people on staff.

- Choose your target. Do you want to aim for Certified, Silver, Gold, or Platinum?

- Decide whether to get formally certified. LEED certification isn't mandatory. Some builders and developers use LEED for design guidance and create buildings that are as green as possible without applying for the LEED certification.

LEED certification doesn't guarantee a high-performance building. The level of LEED certification doesn't in itself ensure better performance—in fact, some LEED Silver buildings have tested more efficient than comparable LEED Gold buildings—but it's a great starting point. How a building is operated has a major impact on efficiency. To get the best possible results, you need to integrate your design choices with user needs for building functionality and maximum performance.

TRUTH

34

The cost of green building

Consider two similar office buildings. One was built traditionally—a developer hired an architect to draw up plans, a construction company built the offices to specifications, and an engineering company installed lighting, temperature control, and water systems. The building serves its purpose just fine, but some workers complain about the air conditioner being too cold, that the air inside feels stuffy, and the office lighting feels "too artificial." The second building was constructed by an integrated design-build-engineering team and was meticulously planned. It uses 30 percent less energy and water than the first building. The building is full of fresh air and natural light, and workers miss fewer days due to illness. In fact, workers are proud to tell friends about their innovative "green" office building.

Which building cost more to build? Most people assume that a superior product costs a lot more and ask, "So how much extra will green cost me?" The more sophisticated question is, "How soon will that extra cost get paid back?" But leading developers are now constructing high-performance green buildings at construction costs similar to traditional buildings—or even lower. (Making the truly sophisticated question more like: "How can we design a building that delivers better performance, lower operating costs, and lower initial costs?")

Think it's more expensive? Think again!—Despite the common perception that green building costs more, building green can help reduce your operating costs with little or no additional construction cost. Numerous examples prove that green building can be cost-effective. In 2003, California's Sustainable Building Task Force published "The Costs and Financial Benefits of Green Buildings," a survey of 33 green buildings for which detailed financial data was available on both traditional and green scenarios. "The eight LEED Bronze buildings had an average cost premium of less than 1 percent. The eighteen Silver buildings averaged a 2.1 percent

How can we design a building that delivers better performance, lower operating costs, and lower initial costs?

...building green can help reduce your operating costs with little or no additional construction cost.

cost premium, whereas the six Gold buildings had an average premium of 1.8 percent. The single Platinum building was at 6.5 percent." The report concluded that the average premium for all 33 studied green buildings was slightly less than 2 percent ($3 to $5 per square foot),[1] an insignificant premium—actually, a great investment—compared with the savings achieved from lower energy and water bills.

Reduced electricity, gas, and water demands create significant savings over the lifetime of a building. For example, the Herman Miller office building in Zeeland, MI—a LEED Gold building built at no incremental cost—uses 31 percent less water and 29 percent less energy than a comparable standard building. Herman Miller expects to see operational cost savings of $1,001,000 at this 95,000-square-foot property over its seven-year lease.

What do you need to know?—Cost-effective green buildings can be achieved by taking an integrative, "whole building approach." The secret is in the planning.

As the Rocky Mountain Institute writes,

"The goal of green building is not to squeeze energy-efficiency features into a tight development budget. The goal, rather, is to analyze such interconnected issues as site and building design, energy and water efficiency, resource efficient construction, lighting and mechanical design, and building ecology, and optimize all these aspects in an integrated design (see Truth 36, "Integrative design for green building"). Features that might have higher individual costs (for example, better windows) might actually reduce the whole building cost because other elements such as the heating system can be downsized or eliminated. To capture these multiple benefits of synergistic design elements, the building must be evaluated as a whole, not "value engineered" item by item.[2]

The itemized cost analysis that RMI warns against is exactly how buildings have traditionally been assessed. It takes a lot more up-front vision and planning to coordinate all the elements in planning phases.

Often the most significant cost-savings come from increased worker productivity in green buildings. All that extra light and fresh air puts workers in a better mood, benefits their health, and has been shown to decrease sick days (see Truth 35, "Green buildings improve productivity").

Considering green building options—There are a number of considerations you should think about:

- Engage your financial team in a fresh look as it conducts cost-benefit analyses for investment options.

- Consider the life-cycle costs in a whole building approach, not just first costs, to get a true comparison of costs and benefits.

- Start your green planning early! Case studies have shown that the earlier a green building project brings its team together for planning, the more savings that are generated by resource efficiency (see Truth 36).

How will energy price volatility affect the economics of green buildings? I see it this way: The financial performance of green buildings is trending better than historical data because the costs premiums are shrinking or disappearing as architects and builders gain experience, whereas the cost of energy, despite current volatility, is likely to continue to rise. And as the United States takes on market caps on carbon, the demand for—and economics of—green buildings will only get better.

TRUTH

35

Green buildings improve productivity

In 1983, Lockheed Missiles and Space Company constructed a new engineering development and design facility in Sunnyvale, CA—a state-of-the-art, energy-efficient building that incorporated natural lighting and provided a constant supply of fresh air. As predicted, Lockheed saved nearly $500,000 a year on energy bills. However, Lockheed also found an additional, unexpected, and remarkable savings: Absenteeism dropped 15 percent, and workers were 15 percent more productive when they were there. The drop in absenteeism alone paid for the new building in one year—a 100% per year ROI![1]

The Lockheed building was one of the earliest documented cases of the impact of green building on increased worker productivity. Similar gains have been observed at Wal-Mart, Boeing, and ING Bank, among other companies. It's difficult to prove that green buildings are the *sole* cause of the increases in productivity. However, increased fresh air ventilation rates, high-performance temperature control, and decreased exposure to toxic materials are closely related to workers being more alert and getting sick less frequently.

The facts—Poor indoor air quality is a serious health problem. Millions of people annually in the United States are affected by "sick building syndrome," a term used to describe situations in which building occupants experience acute health and comfort effects that appear to be linked to time spent in a building. Workers might experience fatigue, difficulty concentrating, and irritated eyes as a result of poor ventilation, mold and chemical exposure, and poor lighting.

Sick building syndrome poses more than a social cost; it can be a significant, though often hidden, expense to business. When you account for the full cost of each absentee day, including salary and suspended work progress, the economic loss is considerable—estimated to be in the tens of billions of dollars annually.[2]

Also, many companies are finding that green buildings help attract and retain top workers, further boosting productivity. A renovation of the HVAC system, acoustics, and spatial layout at the Pacific Northwest National Laboratory decreased employee turnover by 60 percent in the year following the renovation.[3]

LEED Gold- and Platinum-certified buildings are correlated with a 1.5 percent gain in occupant health and productivity. This is a conservative estimate based on observed productivity gains, which ranged from 0.5 percent to 34 percent. A gain of 1.5 percent in productivity is equal to about 7 minutes per day.

...many companies are finding that green buildings help attract and retain top workers....

Over the course of a year, this represents more than a full week of additional productivity per employee—enough to make a significant dent in occupancy costs.[4]

Protecting productivity—Designing buildings is beyond the scope of this book. But here are some guidelines to keep in mind in conversations with architects, facility managers, or leasing agents.

- Choose construction materials and interior finish products with zero or low emissions (volatile organic compounds, or VOCs) to improve indoor air quality.

- Provide adequate ventilation. Building codes generally have minimum rates of ventilation, but green buildings usually exceed these rates. Ventilation systems can be mechanical or passive. Some buildings have CO_2 sensors that set ventilation systems into action to optimize the oxygen levels inside.

- Keep air intakes away from exhaust areas! Surprisingly, this common sense, but often overlooked, design guideline is a common cause of sick building syndrome.

- Provide adequate filtration—install ventilation systems with devices that take harmful particulates and pollutants out of the air.

- Prevent indoor mold through selection of materials resistant to microbial growth, and control humidity.

- Enable occupants to control their environment by installing operable windows and personal workstation climate controls. A University of California at Berkeley study shows that workers are more comfortable when they can control their workplace temperature.[5]

- Ensure that maintenance crews use nontoxic cleaning materials because many building cleaning products are caustic or emit gases, such as VOCs and formaldehyde, that affect health and well-being. Start with your own purchasing department. Whether it buys supplies for your maintenance crew or contracts with an outside janitorial service, request—or insist—that they use nontoxic or "green" cleaning supplies (see Truth 29, "Environmentally preferable purchasing"). Find certified products, including safe cleaning materials, paints, and finishes, at Green Seal.[6]

- Before signing a lease, verify whether the building was constructed using nontoxic materials and whether the cleaning service uses green cleaning supplies.

- Include health concerns and indoor air quality in the building commissioning process. Be sure to request post-construction testing to make sure heating, air conditioning, and lighting systems work properly and efficiently.

TRUTH

36

Integrative design for green building

Typical buildings are created in a piecemeal process—find a site, draw a plan, construct, and then add some mechanical systems. Each phase is optimized independently for speedy completion and low cost. It works, but it leaves money on the table, because optimizing the elements can suboptimize the building.

Simply put, integrative design is a way to break that mold and create truly green, high-performance, healthy buildings. Integrative building design is

> "a process of design in which multiple disciplines and seemingly unrelated aspects of design are integrated in a manner that permits synergistic benefits to be realized. The goal is to achieve high performance and multiple benefits at a lower cost than the total for all the components combined."[1]

This is not the typical way modern buildings are created. The key difference is in the *process*: bringing together all relevant stakeholders early, for a comprehensive consideration of the project. It moves away from the typical model where one team does design, another does mechanical systems, another designs electricity, and so on. It requires more time (and expense) at early stages, but through design synergies and the huge value of getting everyone on the same page, it can speed design, development, construction, and permitting. Going slow to go fast can deliver a better performing building at lower total cost.

Bill Reed of Integrative Design Collaborative says, "The shift from a fragmented worldview to a whole systems mental model is the significant leap our culture must make—framing and understanding living system interrelationships in an integrated way."

In an integrative design process, creative solutions address multiple needs. For example, a traditional building process might ensure a desired temperature range for a building by having an HVAC engineer design a heating system sized to the expected demands for a building of given size, type, and use. However, an HVAC engineer working actively with the architect and the finance team might reach the conclusion that a building design that emphasizes sunlight for heating and air flows for cooling is a more cost-effective solution. Because the integrative process is the driving philosophy behind good green building, it can help guide a project not only toward a certification such as LEED, but can also create efficiencies beyond those prescribed in green building guidelines.

Integrative design is an iterative process. Bill Reed writes, "The process of optimizing each system and part in relation to the whole requires more than a few iterations of thinking. Since we work within the framework of time—a linear process—we need to approximate the simultaneity of the whole by rapid and frequent iteration of ideas."[2]

The earlier an integrated design process is implemented, the more likely you are to find synergistic efficiencies that save you money on operations. Implementing a design process early also increases the likelihood that you can trim construction costs. The later you start the integrated process, the more expensive it becomes to make changes to the building plans. Earlier integration of the design process typically yields better environmental performance as well.

Support integrated design with integrated financial management, using life-cycle costing. Traditional cost estimates focus on the construction costs and fail to incorporate costs of occupancy, such as energy costs or even labor. Costs of occupancy are a significant part of the lifetime cost of a building.

It can be difficult to find team members with experience in integrative design, meaning that the design phase can include lots of time to educate the team on the subject. However, more architecture and construction firms are using integrative design techniques.

"Everyone. Everything. Early."—Here are some tips for putting integrative design into action:

■ Kick off the integrative design process with a "design charette." This intensive, collaborative design session—with a full complement of stakeholders and every aspect of the project on the table—helps ensure that you work as a team, with full consideration of all relevant factors, right from the start. In Bill Reed's words: "Everyone. Everything. Early." The charette is a good way to communicate and clarify green goals for the project and to turn your group of specialists into a true team with common goals. Your list of people to invite to the team should include architects, engineers, finance, operations team, and legal.

The charette should generate a compelling, shared story to guide the design team and the client.

- Assess the site and your building needs. Or more accurately, assess the needs of the people that will occupy the building. How will you use water, energy, living systems, and materials to meet those needs? (You'll do some of this as preparation for the charette, and some during it.)

- Set initial goals for your green building. But don't limit yourself to a shopping list of features and technologies. Start with performance goals, including energy and water benchmarks, and let the lists follow, not drive, the process. Research other green building case studies for some inspiration. Think about how you can go beyond "doing less harm" to building something that actually enhances natural capital.

- After the charette and buy-in from decision makers, the design team should discuss how it will approach the actual building process. Architects should create specific designs for the entire team to review and refine. Continual, active communications among the various specialists is key; effective communication helps make sure the building is properly calibrated for all systems.

- Schedule frequent team workshops after the initial charette and early phases of work. A standard building has one workshop, and the integrative design process can have upward of five.

TRUTH

37

Computers and electronics

Computers, servers, and networks use energy, generate heat, affect building energy use, and move some unpleasant materials around the planet. What options do we have to use and make the technology we depend on differently?

What's in that box?—Computers and electronics keep shrinking but still have a large footprint—from their manufacture and transportation (usually from overseas), energy consumption during use (which dwarfs the energy in manufacture and transport), and disposal. Final assembly is relatively simple and not chemically intensive, but chip production, circuit board etching, and mercury injection for LCD screens have far more environmental and human impact.

Computers keep shrinking but still have a large footprint.

At the end of the computer's "useful" life, or when a new model is released, the product is at the threshold of entering a waste stream where the embedded toxins could leach from landfill to water tables, or be reused or recycled.

What's in your trash?—E-waste in the United States totals 2.9 million tons per year—more than 1 percent of the solid waste stream. Every day, 112,000 computers are discarded and 88.6% of all U.S. e-waste (also called e-scrap) is landfilled or incinerated.[1]

One percent of the waste stream might seem insignificant, but many of the chemicals in e-waste are extremely hazardous to living systems.

Every day, 112,000 computers are discarded....

Lead, cadmium, brominated flame retardants, phosphorus, barium, dioxin, mercury, beryllium, hexavalent chromium, and polyvinyl chloride are some of the toxins found in the average computer and monitor. (You find less of these substances in some newer computers and monitors because the EU now restricts many of them in electronics products.)

Computers have become more energy-efficient in recent years (with still-significant differences in consumption between manufacturers

154

and models), but the energy demand of all the computers and servers at your company can add up to real money.

Use the right purchasing criteria—It's worth giving some thought to your purchasing criteria for computers and electronic equipment. (I'll discuss servers in Truth 38, "Creating more efficient data centers.")

- Purchase energy-efficient computers—look for the EnergyStar logo.

- Buy upgradeable computers, so you can maximize the performance of your existing machine without having to replace it outright in the future.

- Use energy-efficient liquid crystal display (LCD) or light emitting diode (LED) monitors, designated with an EnergyStar logo.

- Buy the right computer for the job. Powerful graphics cards can use more electricity, and employees who mostly use email and word processing don't need the same processing power that design software or video processing needs.

- Buy recyclable and refurbished products—from companies that use less toxic and hazardous materials. Dell has made commitments to increasing the recycled content in its products, Hewlett-Packard has a robust take-back recycling program, and energy-efficient Fujitsu Siemens computers are available on the European market—with PC boards made without lead.[2] Check out Greenpeace Guide to Greener Electronics, which some credit for driving the major eco-improvements made recently by Apple.

Use your computers wisely—Buying smart is the first step. There's also opportunity in how you use the equipment you buy:

- Make sure the sleep and power save modes are turned on! This is a surprisingly common oversight that your network administrator can handle centrally for all your computers.

- Set computers to enter standby or hibernate modes after 30 to 60 minutes of inactivity; set monitors to sleep after five to 20 minutes of inactivity.[3]

- Use "thin client" or remote desktop computing, which requires minimal computing power on the desk for user interface and does its main processing on a networked server, or "in the cloud."

Benefits include less expensive hardware for end users, less risk of losing data, and consolidation of maintenance, repairs, and software upgrades.

- Telecommute. When Sun Microsystems used its thin client systems to support an intensive telecommuting initiative, it not only cut the per employee energy use in half while reducing environmental impacts from employee commutes—but it also saved $68 million a year in real estate costs![4]

- Dispose of components properly and participate in product take-back (see Truth 21, "Product take-back"). Many jurisdictions (California and the EU, to name two) consider computers hazardous waste. It's illegal to just throw them away.

- Estimate how much you're spending to run your computers, and make the total cost of operations (TCO) case to your manager, purchasing staff, and IT department to invest in greener computers. Learn more at these sites:

Greenpeace Guide to Greener Electronics: www.greenpeace.org/usa/assets/binaries/guide-to-greener-electronics.

ACEEE Online Guide to Energy-Efficient Commercial Equipment: http://www.aceee.org/ogeece/ch5_office.htm.

Electronics Council: www.greenelectronicscouncil.org.

Silicon Valley Toxics Coalition: www.etoxics.org/site/PageServer.

National Geographic: E-Waste, http://ngm.nationalgeographic.com/geopedia/E-Waste.

The Rise of Bright Green Computers, by Jer Faludi at *WorldChanging*: www.worldchanging.com/archives/004350.html.

TRUTH
38

Creating more efficient
data centers

When Google decided to go green, one of its key goals was to become carbon neutral. This meant addressing energy consumption in its data center—a major contributor to its environmental footprint and its operating costs (see Truth 14, "Carbon footprinting"). The company has since become a pioneer in engineering efficient data centers.[1]

Reducing footprints and saving money—Modern commerce depends on data that is stored and processed in large, power-hungry computer data centers that use between 1.2 to 2.0 percent of the electricity consumed in the United States, creating a significant carbon footprint and requiring ever-more generating capacity from the grid.[2]

To reduce that footprint—and the energy spent associated with it—companies are putting a great deal of effort into designing and operating more-efficient data centers. These data centers use more efficient chips and fans, better computers, and better arrangements of computers within their buildings. However, there are still many opportunities to optimize those data centers and run them more efficiently. In fact, Amory Lovins, Chairman and Chief Scientist at Rocky Mountain Institute, says data centers can cut power use by 89 percent.[3]

Greening your data center also can save significant money. The average data center has annual energy costs 15 times as much as conventional office buildings on a square foot basis, and some are

> …you might be spending more to operate IT systems than you paid to buy them.

more than 40 times as expensive.[4] Factor in rising energy costs and the monetization of carbon emissions, and you might be spending as much to operate IT systems than you paid to buy them. (IDC estimates that 50 cents is spent on powering and cooling data centers for every dollar spent on new data center hardware.[5])

It's not just about the energy used by the machines. Rising demand for data centers puts a growing demand on energy infrastructure, requiring upgrades, increased capacity, and additional facilities. Data centers generate a lot of heat, which adds load to building cooling systems, requiring additional energy and facility upgrades.

Greening your data centers—
There's a large and growing amount of literature about green data centers, but here are a few key steps that any initiatives should include:

Rising demand for data centers puts a growing demand on energy infrastructure....

- Start by evaluating your current data centers. Use your energy bills or check usage rates on your machines to determine how much energy you currently use.

- Monitor energy usage and thermal profiles to identify "hot spots," which can affect performance and energy consumption for cooling.

- Use power management software. "In a typical data center, the electricity usage hardly varies at all, but the IT load varies by a factor of three or more. That tells you that we're not properly implementing power management," says Amory Lovins.[6] Power management is incorporated in newer systems, but make sure it's active (because surprisingly often, power management is disabled in system settings) for both data centers and computers (see Truth 37, "Computers and electronics").

- Reduce energy costs and consumption through both physical consolidation and virtualization. Most servers and desktops today are in use only 8 percent to 15 percent of the time they are powered on, yet consume as much as 60 percent to 90 percent of the normal workload power even when idle. In a major overhaul, Sun Microsystems consolidated 2,177 servers on 500 racks down to 1,240 servers on 65 racks. The move reduced power consumption by 75 percent and increased computing power by about four times.[7]

- Determine who makes IT and funding decisions at your company and explore total cost of operations (TCO) options for optimizing your equipment or upgrading to more-efficient equipment.

- When you eventually need new equipment, make sure you get the most-efficient technology. Where possible, upgrade and repurpose the old equipment before buying new gear. Likewise, buy equipment that is easy to upgrade in the future.

- Use innovative technology and design. Consider liquid cooling technology, with reclaimed, nonpotable water if possible. Use combined heat and power systems; for example, use "waste" heat from servers to provide other energy needs. Network Appliances, a Sunnyvale, CA-based data management firm, uses a natural-gas-powered cogeneration system during peak hours when electricity rates increase. It saves about $300,000 a year in energy costs while also providing a source of "free cooling" for the data center.[8]

- If you're building a new data center or new building, use integrative design (see Truth 36, "Integrative design for green building") to plan for data centers early in the design process and open up opportunities to significantly shrink operating costs. Buildings and rooms can be built to cool data centers with natural ventilation or water, and data centers can be located far from areas such as offices that need to be cool in the summer.

TRUTH

39

How IT can drive greening

"As far as we know, there's nothing more powerful in the universe than 6 billion minds wrapping around a problem," says Amory Lovins, Chairman and Chief Scientist at Rocky Mountain Institute.[1] Ask most people concerned with sustainability about the relationship between information technology and sustainability, and they'll probably talk about the increasing electricity load of computers and data centers (see Truth 37, "Computers and electronics," and Truth 38, "Creating more efficient data centers") or the toxic materials in e-waste. But there's an equally important upside: the contribution IT can make to a more sustainable world.

IT products and services—servers to software to sensors—can monitor (in real time) and manage resource use from home energy consumption and industrial wastewater flows to the environmental footprint of retail products. They provide increasingly precise information that can inform companies, communities, and consumers about the true sustainability of every aspect of their lives and activities, and guide them—often in effortless ways—to better environmental and economic choices and performance.

Sustainable IT—For businesses, sustainable IT means bringing awareness to risks and opportunities previously hidden from view. For individuals, sustainable IT means clearly seeing one's own consumption and one's relationship to others. For all of us, well-aimed information technology is key to realizing these possibilities.

IT can help you become leaner and greener, with real-time feedback that lets you adjust and continually improve your performance. Ask anyone who has driven a Toyota Prius about the impact the miles per gallon dashboard has on driving behavior.

IT can help you become leaner and greener, with real-time feedback that lets you adjust and continually improve your performance.

How to use IT for green—Here are some steps to consider:

- **Measure what matters**—As carbon tracking becomes the language of the business and sustainability intersection, metrics that track a company's environmental performance become increasingly important. Providing a real-time view of sustainability trends and productivity ratios, and making it easy to compare performance between facilities and between companies, helps businesses make smarter decisions and deliver both lower footprint and higher profit. Innovest's Carbon Beta™ is just one example of how Wall Street is beginning to correlate environmental risk and financial risk with computer models that carefully analyze and juxtapose data from both realms. Natural Logic's Business Metabolics™ dashboard systems[2] streamline the task of tracking sustainability performance, and turn the static, "rear-view" mirror process of corporate social responsibility (CSR) reporting into an interactive management tool.

- **Use IT to dematerialize**—Amazon.com is perhaps the largest example of IT-driven dematerialization. Highly automated warehousing and cataloging software allows the company to operate without energy-intensive stores. Apple's iTunes digital music store takes the dematerialization model a step further. Apple still has some overhead costs (such as licensing and equipment), but there are no stores, warehouses, or physical product.

- **Use IT to support telecommuting**—Sun Microsystems used routing software to optimize ride-sharing and shuttle services and get employees out of their cars. Commuting accounted for more than 98 percent of each employee's work-related carbon footprint.[3] With IT and thin-client computing, Sun saves energy from building use, saves employees money on commuting, and downsizes its real estate requirements.

- **Use IT to implement "just in time" and lean practices**—"Just in time" production requires sophisticated systems to tightly coordinate inventory, cycle time, and work schedules to minimize waste of all kinds throughout the process (see Truth 13, "Running lean and green"). IT (when properly designed and deployed—it's not a panacea!) can amplify your commitment to provide adaptable tools that support the work of the people who are at the core of your enterprise.

- **Use IT for green building**—Occupancy sensors are one small but significant example of the greening—and smartening—of our buildings (see Truths 33–36 about green building). When equipment and climate control systems are networked and tracked by monitoring software that optimizes system loads and power consumption, comfort and light can be maintained at a fraction of the cost—and with a fraction of the electricity and GHGs—previously required.

- **Use IT for life-cycle assessment**—Tracking the life-cycle impact of products is central to furniture manufacturer Herman Miller's business. Designers use the environmental impact of the manufacturing materials to guide strategic decisions that impact profits, consumers, and the planet. The IT systems and materials databases used by HM makes the time-consuming work of tracking LCA data an easy part of the design process (see Truth 20, "What makes a product green?").

TRUTH

Engaging employees

Building your green strategy into the daily life of your business means changes in behavior, not just technology. But how do you get your employees aboard? How do you get your employees to embrace and implement your company's green mission? And how does the "We've always done it this way" sentiment change?

These are essential questions because highly engaged employees outperform their disengaged colleagues by 20 percent to 28 percent, according to a 2006 Conference Board report.[1] A 2004 study of 28 multinational companies found that the share prices of organizations with highly engaged employees rose three times faster than industry averages.[2]

Clean technology gets a lot of attention, but people are the heart of greening a company. People—staff at all levels, not just managers—hold valuable knowledge about how a company operates, what works, and what doesn't. Their knowledge is as important as their participation in green teams. What people do each day is where the DNA of your company (its culture and its policies and operating procedures) is "expressed." Changing the DNA is one thing; having that show up as different behavior on the ground—in everything from purchasing to design to customer service—is quite another.

How to engage your employees—Engaging your employees—really engaging them, not just paying lip service to the notion—takes thoughtfulness, commitment, heart, and, above all, respect.

- Know the value. Managers often assume they can't afford to engage their employees, but the value of an employee who knows the right thing to do—or how to figure out what that is—outweighs the effort needed to engage them. Employees who are engaged in greening create value through added efficiency, waste reduction, and process improvement.

> ...greening your business is something to do *with* your employees, not *to* them.

- Know that greening your business is something to do *with* your employees, not *to* them. Many clients ask us about "training" their staff, but in truth it's more about learning than training.

- Know that change does happen, but it's a bit like the old joke: "How many psychiatrists does it take to change a light bulb? Just one, but the light bulb's got to really want to change."

- Get everyone on same page. A shared mental model, like the Natural Step (TNS) management framework (see Truth 9, "Secrets hiding in plain sight"), provides a common sense of direction and a shared vocabulary for discovering new opportunities. When Ikea trained its entire workforce in the TNS framework, it was surprised to find suggestion boxes stuffed to the brim with good ideas.

- Listen to your employees—even ones you might not think of as innovative. When the Scandic hotel chain engaged its workforce in learning and working with the TNS framework, management was surprised to find that many of the best ideas came from the chambermaids; they weren't highly educated, but they were "face to customer," and once equipped with the right questions, they saw things that no one else could see.

- Start a green team, representing a cross-section of the company, with different functions and levels of seniority. Get management support if at all possible—if only to give your green champions some free time to drive the process. (Look what a gold mine 3M's "15% rule," which encourages people to spend 15 percent of their time on projects of their own choosing, has been for that company's patent pipeline!)[3] But be prepared to proceed and show value as informal "skunkworks" if management isn't ready.

- Build greening efforts into your employees' job tasks. Let them know how they can contribute. The payoff to the company is clear, so enable them to spend time on green initiatives.

- Communicate the results, including both successes and failures. Case studies and demonstrated cost-savings are effective tools in communicating the value and results of employee initiatives.

- Show the results directly, whether in management reports, control charts, or performance dashboards, so people can see how their "drop in the bucket," in the words of David Gershon, helps fill the bucket (see Truth 42, "Keeping score").

- Let employees know that their opinions and efforts matter, and reward their contributions. Use the right incentives because different people will be motivated by different things (see Truth 43, "Employee incentives"). One thing is clear, however—everyone's busy, so you need to be clear about why they should bother with helping green their company.

The bigger picture—This isn't just about profit. It's also about impacting people's lives by giving them control in their jobs and their impact on the environment (for example, Wal-Mart's personal sustainability plans challenge employees to make changes in their personal lives and their work lives).

That kind of engaged employee isn't just good for the employee—though it certainly is. It might be the best thing for your profit, too.

TRUTH

41

Engaging stakeholders

A few years ago, former Natural Logic VP Bill Reed worked with a group of stakeholders around a school expansion project. Neighbors loved the school, but the Not in My Backyard (NIMBY) sentiment was winning the day, and lawyers for all sides were sharpening their knives...uh, briefs. Bill managed to lock everyone in a room for two days and gradually peeled away the positions to the underlying concerns, found common ground, and *then* began design. The result? A better school with far better energy and water efficiency, a zoning variance in months from a county that hadn't granted one in years, years of litigation and delay avoided—and a community at peace instead of at war.

Business ethicist R. Edward Freeman theorized that business has a duty to serve not only its shareholders by increasing profits, but also to increase value to all stakeholders.[1] Environmental performance is an important player in delivering value (clean air, natural resources) to stakeholders.

> No one has a monopoly on wisdom in a rapidly changing world.

Some view this as a moral concern. I see it as a management imperative.

No one has a monopoly on wisdom in a rapidly changing world. "None of us is as smart as all of us," as green designer Carroll Moore likes to say, so we need all hands on deck—employees, customers, supply chain partners, and investors. All have opinions, information, insight, and influence on how you operate, an ability to help or thwart your initiatives, and a stake in your results. Engaging this diverse group of stakeholders is now a critical business skill.

Some companies think of environmental stakeholders as opponents they need to appease, but active, engaged stakeholders can provide added value and momentum. Hewlett-Packard is one of many companies that have formed a stakeholders council with NGO representatives and corporate executives to stay abreast of upcoming citizenship issues, based on the belief that global citizenship creates financial value rather than simply satisfying charitable commitments.[2]

How to engage your stakeholders—Engaging your stakeholders requires a little bit of courage and a lot of integrity.

Engaging this diverse group of stakeholders is now a critical business skill

- Know who your stakeholders are. List people, organizations, communities, and life forms that are likely to be affected by your project. Include suppliers, employees, and customers, as well as local property owners, businesses, governments, and nonprofits. Be expansive and inclusive, and try to identify groups that are typically overlooked. (It can be helpful to think visually: Draw the relationships on the wall, rather than just list them on a computer.)

- Know which stakeholders are key on which issues. Trying to engage everyone on everything might spread your efforts thin. Think about which ones are most strongly affected, those who hold influence, who are accessible, and who are willing to engage, and which ones hold valuable information.

- Get your stakeholders in the loop. Don't just ask them to comment on plans you've already made; you'll lose both their interest and potential value. You'll get better results when you seek input before your plans are set, while their ideas can still make a difference, and while potential issues are still design options rather than points of contention. Doing so can help keep you out of pitfalls you haven't seen and surface opportunities you might have missed. Bill Reed's watchwords: "Everybody. Everything. Early."

- Invite your initial list of stakeholders to introduce you to new key stakeholders.

- Provide a way for stakeholder voices to be heard. Hewlett-Packard holds stakeholder meetings twice a year to get input on how it's performing and what might be on the horizon.

- Be patient. External stakeholders might be accustomed to an adversarial relationship, especially with environmental issues. Turn that relationship on its head to truly include stakeholders, and you're more likely to have a productive conversation. But it might take time to build trust.

The key: Make it real, not just lip service.

■ The key: Make it real, not just lip service. Sincerely engage people and follow through on your commitments. Remember, a stakeholder relationship is like any relationship; if it's to thrive, you need to be open to being changed.

TRUTH

Keeping score

When Natural Logic evaluated operations at environmental leader Odwalla many years ago, we found a surprising fact. Despite a company policy to buy recycled content paper (see Truth 29, "Environmentally preferable purchasing"), and enthusiastic support from employees, very little of the paper they bought had much recycled content. Each buyer confessed that they occasionally had to make exceptions to the policy, but they were sure that everyone else was staying with the program. Except they weren't....

Our intervention was simple. No exhortations, trainings, or rewards (see Truth 43, "Employee incentives") were given. Instead, we created a simple chart to post on every buyer's wall graphically showing the last period's results. The next time we checked back, the trend was reversed. Most of the paper purchased had *high* recycled content. This was a little lesson in the power of keeping score, and what I call "generative feedback."

Everyone knows that "what gets measured gets done." Well, not exactly, but the opposite is certainly true—you can't manage what you don't measure. But how do you select *powerful* measures and goals that help drive better decisions, and better performance? And how do you put those measures to work for your organization?

Give your company "self-control"—JM Juran, one of the creators of Total Quality Management, observed in 1948 that "to be in a state of 'self-control,' a person needs to know what is expected, what resources are available, and how well [s]he is doing to meet those expectations. If *any* of those three is lacking," he noted, "a person is not in a state of self-control, and cannot be held responsible" for his or her actions.

Juran's 60-year-old observation defines the management challenge we still face today:

- To provide people with relevant, timely, accurate, and meaningful information
- That helps them make consistently better decisions
- So their autonomous actions support larger institutional goals
- Without drowning them in data overload

Unfortunately, few people that I speak with, even at exceptional companies, say they meet all three of Juran's conditions. Many don't meet even one.

Select relevant indicators from the data stew—The challenge is that there are a million things you could measure—well, at least dozens—but people don't pay real attention to more than a few. Here's how we help our clients select "the measures that matter:"

- Gather a cross-functional team from your company—and, ideally, key stakeholders to design an effective and implementable goals/indicators/metrics system. Each brings a different perspective, and only with all those perspectives is a sufficiently complete view possible.

- Map your key metabolic flows. Trace key resources as they pass through your company's processes, to develop an inventory of the flows you might possibly measure.

- Rank the aspects of each flow, as you would when creating an EMS (see Truth 44, "Environmental management systems"). Which ones have significant environmental impacts, such as carbon intensity or toxicity, or business impacts like capital expenditures or operating costs, or pose a material risk (supply bottlenecks, regulatory risk, and others)?

- Distill the key performance indicators (KPIs) that add insight for your strategic and operational decision makers. Determine which factors are what we call "the measures that matter."

- Design data collection systems that allow you to measure them in a systematic, manageable, and economical way which gets accurate information to the right people at the right time.

- Communicate results to stakeholders. Many companies produce annual CSR reports, which is a step in the right direction but often little more than an expensive press release. In addition, use your IT systems to deliver well-chosen KPIs to the right people at the right time—monthly or even daily, instead of annually—to help them make better business decisions *right now*[1] (see Truth 39, "How IT can drive greening").

- Compare your performance with your peers and competitors— internally and externally. We find that this collaborative

175

...the "we're doing as well as can be done" sentiment just isn't going to fly any more.

benchmarking is one of the best ways to get people motivated to change. If another division or another company is performing better that yours, then the "we're doing as well as can be done" sentiment just isn't going to fly anymore.

- Think about what you measure, and why. Are your reporting systems a rear-view mirror, documenting what's happened? Or are your reporting systems a radar system that can help you affect what's going to happen? We call it "generative feedback"— performance feedback that doesn't just track behavior; it drives it by changing the way people talk and think about performance.

TRUTH

43

Employee incentives

While rolling out a recycling program for a large transportation client, Natural Logic's Nick Kordesch discussed incentives for the amount of waste diverted by the team. Most employees were interested in pitching in with the new program, but each responded to different messages. One wanted a celebration BBQ with the team. Another was looking forward to telling his kids about the effort. A group in the back had their eyes on the prize—Oakland Raiders construction helmets. One of the green team champions beamed when the team leader praised his efforts in front of the team. The point: different strokes for different folks.

Greening your business isn't just about changing technology; it also depends on changing behavior so that your people do different things—the right thing—on Monday morning. But changing behavior isn't always easy. Have you ever tried to change a habit? Or a spouse's habit?

So we're faced with the question of "what motivates change?"

When people talk about changing behavior—of companies and the people who constitute them—they often talk first about incentives. It does take something to overcome habits, but does it take incentives? And if so, does it take financial incentives?

I say, "Not necessarily."

Both policymakers and activists tend to have a knee-jerk reaction toward financial incentives such as tax credits (externally) and bonuses (internally) as a first step in trying to influence behavior. Similarly, employers often think financial rewards are the best ways to motivate employees. I see incentives as a useful tool in the toolbox, but not the place to start. Why?

> I see incentives as a useful tool in the toolbox, but not the place to start.

To be successful, you need as many parties on board as possible. To get them on board, you need to use the right incentives and methods to motivate them.

Offering the right incentives—People and businesses with different motivation respond to different incentives. Engaging your employees is an essential part of jump-starting green initiatives. Rewarding people for recycling is fine, but getting them to think about how they can improve business and the environment is a much more powerful accomplishment. The truth is not all employees are moved solely by money, and not all companies are blocked from green initiatives because of cost. Employees can be engaged by actively informing them, bragging about their accomplishments, and including them in decision making, as well as with financial incentives (see Truth 40, "Engaging employees"). Companies can be motivated by learning to more accurately calculate costs and benefits, and by remembering what they're really here to do (see Truth 6, "Profit and purpose").

Here are some approaches to consider:

- Open a dialogue with employees about green initiatives. Find out what they care about. Just having this conversation often provides an *intrinsic* reward as employees become motivated by being active stakeholders in the process.

- Experiment with a variety of incentives. Think about the different ways you can change behavior. Employees are motivated by peer recognition, learning opportunities and career development, having a voice and control over their job, prizes, making an impact on the environment, or simply appreciation.

- Let employees know the score using generative feedback— performance feedback that doesn't just track behavior; it drives it (see Truth 42, "Keeping score"). We found that this is one of the most powerful ways to encourage behavioral changes. When your people know three key things—what's expected of them, the impacts of their actions, and what they can do to improve their results—they operate more autonomously and perform more effectively. Without these three conditions, JM Juran (one of the founders of Total Quality Management) noted more than 60 years ago, "People are not in a state of self control, and can't be held responsible."[1] Conversely, generative feedback with those three conditions met can drive higher product and yields, and lower defects and absenteeism—without goals, motivation, or "incentives."[2]

- Build shared commitments and common purpose; be wary of incentives that suboptimize performance, by pitting individuals against teams or department goals.

- Don't consider nonfinancial incentives an excuse to pay your employees less and try to motivate them with cheaper methods. Sharing the value that people create—like a stake in profits—is a great motivator, too. And some would say it's the right thing to do.

TRUTH

44

Environmental
management systems

Management systems help companies systematically embed "doing the right thing" into standard, everyday practice. They can save time and money by helping turn good ideas into best practices, and, in turn, into reliably replicable procedures. They can help sales because—as the ISO 9000 standard has done for quality, and the ISO 14000 series is doing for environmental management—they assure your customers that you can consistently produce desired results.

An *Environmental Management System (EMS)* is a set of processes and practices that enables an organization to systematize management of its environmental impacts and increase its operating efficiency.[1]

An EMS can help make your environmental practices more transparent, so you can streamline your customers' auditing processes and communicate to employees, management, and shareholders that you are practicing sound environmental management.

An EMS can give you a higher bar to aim for....

An EMS can give you a higher bar to aim for and help embed that bar into your standard business practices (see Truth 32, "Clearing the rising bar"). You can build your processes to consistently meet your EMS's specifications instead of hoping that you meet a "minimum tolerance level" for compliance.

Know the standards—The International Organization for Standardization (ISO), the source of the ISO 9000 international quality standard, created the "14000 family of standards" for Environmental Management:[2]

- ISO 14001: Environmental Management Systems Requirements
- ISO 14004: Implementation Guidelines
- ISO 14010–14015: Environmental Auditing
- ISO 14024: Environmental Labeling
- ISO 14031: Environmental Performance Evaluation
- ISO 14040–14044: Life Cycle Analysis
- ISO 14050: Terms and Definitions

- ISO 14060: Inclusion of Environmental Aspects in Product Standards

- ISO 19011: Auditing 14000 and 9000

Creating an EMS—An EMS should embed into operating practices a continual cycle of planning, implementing, reviewing, and improving the processes and actions that an organization undertakes to meet its business and environmental goals.

The basic steps for creating an EMS follow the familiar Plan/Do/ Check/Act quality cycle:

- **Plan (Design):** Identify the company's environmental "aspects"— the impacts of its activities, products, and services—and establish goals to improve them. Key actions include securing commitments from top management and finding an "EMS Champion."

- **Do (Implement):** Designate responsibilities and train your staff. The more your people—top to bottom—understand about the environmental impacts of their actions, the more they can contribute to a process of continual improvement. Prepare EMS Documentation (Manual).

- **Check (Measure):** Monitor performance and identify corrective actions (see Truth 42, "Keeping score").

- **Act (Review):** Perform regular progress reviews and make needed changes to the EMS document.

Get the most from your EMS—Creating an EMS is one thing. Using it effectively, to build business value, is another. Here are some steps to consider:

- Focus on results. The EMS framework focuses on process and is outcome-agnostic; in theory, you could build a certified management system that delivers meager though consistent results. Instead, use the power of management systems to drive toward significant improvement in a systematic way.

- Leverage your management system by tracking costs of implementation and quantifying its benefits, to support the business case to company leadership for continued investment in further improvement.

- Use *Environmental Management Information Systems (EMIS)* to embed feedback into your management systems (see Truth 42).

- Don't obsess about certification. A well-implemented EMS—just like a LEED-compliant building (see Truth 33, "LEED standards for green buildings")—has intrinsic business value, whether you decide to seek formal certification (which is a separate business decision based on your customers' needs).

Don't confuse the tool with the goal—Standards, as valuable as they are for at least ensuring baseline consistency of practice, and sometimes ensuring that often-forgotten issues at least get systematically considered, are no substitute for other important virtues such as innovation, continuous improvement, and a consistent, focused impact on business value.

TRUTH

45

Profit, value, and risk

Swiss Re and Munich Re, the world's largest reinsurance companies, are all about risk. So how do they approach the challenge of climate change? In effect, they have said, "We're not scientists, but based on our actuarial analysis, we can't afford the risk of even the possibility that the science is right. The scale of potential damage is so large that even a small risk is already unacceptable." That's why these "conservative" companies are driving greenhouse gas reduction programs at the companies they insure.

Business regularly miscalculates risk and benefit, as the result of a structural inability to accurately assign value to factors that are material—significant but not yet monetized (rendered as numbers on financial reports).

Overlooked value and risk hover at the intersection of the human economy and the economy of nature that supports it—excluded from our economic system as externalities but eventually showing up to bite us as market distortions. Although it might seem rational to ignore them in the short term, these excluded values and risks impact your company's performance, readiness, and resilience. Here are some of the places where you can find them:

- **Profit**—Improving efficiency, reducing non-product, and eliminating waste, and turning former costs centers into future profit centers

Business regularly miscalculates risk and benefit....

- **Value**—The resilience of living systems and the services they provide.

- **Risks**—Resource costs and reliability of supply, future costs of emissions (GHG and other), rising regulatory bars, license to operate, competitive innovation, market expectations, and so on.

It's your responsibility as a business leader (see Truth 49, "Fiduciary duty") to navigate risks, and build and preserve value. When you can see risk and value that others can't, you're at an advantage. When you can't, you're at a disadvantage. If you ignore material risks that you can see, you could be failing in your duty to your shareholders, your family, and yourself.

Understand the basics—

Understanding and respecting the requirements of the living systems that sustain the human economy is the key. The guidelines are simple, right there in nature's playbook. Current solar income drives the global economy. Living systems operate with closed—and stunningly diverse—cycles of material exchange, where there is no waste, only food. Toxic materials (such as a rattlesnake's venom) are synthesized as needed, not stockpiled or scattered, and never stored or dispersed.

If you ignore material risks that you can see, you could be failing in your duty to your shareholders, your family, and yourself.

When businesses deviate from this time-tested approach, my risk alarms go off—and yours should, too. As for business systems, Former DuPont CFO Gary Pfeiffer's formula for how investors understand sustainability provides a simple guide:

- Increase profits, by
    - Eliminating "waste" (see Truth 11, "Waste? Not! Eliminating non-product").
    - Growing sales by meeting and anticipating emerging market demand.
    - Driving innovation by better understanding both ecological and policy drivers.
- Accelerate the harvest of those profits while
    - Shortening time to market.
    - Propelling your innovation pipeline.
    - Growing product extensions.
- Reduce risk, by
    - Building regulatory "insulation" (and ensuring the ability to play by your rules, not the regulators', while preserving access to key markets).
    - Embracing the responsibility—and opportunity—in managing (for example, taking back) your product and material streams after the end of their officially useful life.

A "sustainability lens" can help you increase and harvest profits by guiding product and service innovation that can profitably meet present and anticipated market needs, meet them sooner than the competition, and turn them profitable faster than the competition. DuPont shifted to selling automakers car painting services instead of paint (reversing their financial incentive by transforming the paint from a revenue source to a cost of production) and drove innovations that reduced VOCs and overspray, because any chemistry that doesn't adhere to the car adds no value to DuPont's customers or their shareholders (see Truth 22, "Product to service").

To reduce risk, you need to control the factors that can threaten or weaken cash flow. This can include barriers to market entry from future regulatory hurdles, missing shifting market expectations or competitor innovations, and facing unanticipated calamities such as Bhopal[1] or fully anticipated ones such as rising sea levels.

Navigating the unseen profit, value, and risk—Business leaders are tasked to navigate the seen and the unseen (see Truth 50, "Certainty in the face of uncertainty"). Companies that have taken up strategic sustainability commitments and have seen what's not yet seen by others (see Truth 9, "Secrets hiding in plain sight") have delivered increased profitability, reduced risk, and positive environmental benefits—all of which contribute to the triple benefits of revenue, continuity of revenue, and the public confidence that can help them increase their revenue.

So think about greening your company not as an environmental issue but as a question of value building and risk management, and ask yourself: "What's our next, bold commitment to reducing risk and building shareholder value?"

TRUTH

Reality-based accounting

One hundred years ago, Oscar Wilde skewered those who "know the price of everything and the value of nothing." He could have been talking about modern business.

Why does the modern economy do so much damage to the environment? Because it operates within the myth of "externalities"—the convenient fiction that things outside the monetary boundaries of our economy are thus out of mind and without "value." In reality, of course, nothing is external. Every material a company produces goes somewhere, even if we pretend it's not there, and has an impact, even if we pretend it doesn't.

Reality-based accounting is the name I've given to the practice of expanding the boundaries of traditional accounting to fully engage physical reality by internalizing externalities—and capturing the true risks and values that traditional accounting excludes. Carbon markets are a step in the right direction, but only

> Every material a company produces goes somewhere, even if we pretend it's not there, and has an impact, even if we pretend it doesn't.

a step (see Truth 48, "Carbon trading and offsets"). We still operate in an economy distorted by unmonetized costs and benefits that amount to, in Robert F. Kennedy Jr.'s words, "a subsidy to polluters for environmental degradation."[1]

Modern accounting is myopically bottom-line focused and, as a result, is deeply flawed. We don't really know how to count—or more precisely, how to take everything into account. Businesses don't merely lose valuable information because of this disconnect from reality—they are literally blind to opportunities that the P&L and balance sheet currently cannot recognize. (One of my editors admonished me not to use "literally blind" because the phrase is metaphoric, not literal. But the fact is, there is information essential to your business that you simply can't see on the balance sheet—it just doesn't show up there. See the following Odwalla example.)

I predict that reality-based accounting will come to be seen as part of fiduciary duty (see Truth 49, "Fiduciary duty") as companies are increasingly required to track and disclose environmental performance and risks. In the meantime, it can provide an early-warning system—and a source of insight and opportunity—for companies that do it now.

Internalize the externalities—This is a big job, and much of it is more a matter of policy than the purview of an individual firm. But there are steps individual companies can take—and that might make currently invisible opportunities visible for you to consider and exploit:

- Understand the physics that underlies the chemistry that underlies the biology that underlies the ecology that underlies the human economy. This can help you think about issues and identify risks that are invisible to your competitors. For example, most companies didn't consider greenhouse gases to be a liability because they were externalized, unregulated, and unpriced. Others, such as chip-maker ST Microelectronics (which issued its "Environmental Decalogue" back in 1995), understood, from the underlying science, that these emissions have a significant impact on the climate and should be accounted for. ST Microelectronics then set about to profitably reduce them, years ahead of almost anyone else.[2]

- Measure your metabolism. Account for your material inputs and physical impacts in addition to your traditional accounting (see Truth 42, "Keeping score"). When Natural Logic conducted an EcoAudit for juice maker Odwalla, we charted resource flows (including energy, water, and commodities), procurement (including recycled content and agricultural production), waste generation, and recycling. This new lens enabled us to find significant profit opportunities in a completely normal wastewater stream, by finding productive uses for valuable nutrients literally being poured down the drain—opportunities that were invisible on standard financial management reports.

- Use those metabolic performance indicators as a parallel set of books—or dashboards—to help your people keep their eyes on

> **Carbon emissions will be on your books soon enough, but don't be limited by what's required; policy usually lags innovation.**

issues that haven't yet made it onto your balance sheet and P&L as part of standard accounting practice. Carbon emissions will be on your books soon enough, but don't be limited by what's required; policy usually lags innovation.

- Widen your circle of concern. Look further upstream and downstream to identify potential operating efficiency improvements, design, and dematerialization opportunities. Consider life-cycle impacts (see Truth 20, "What makes a product green?") of your business—and the opportunities that might open as you do.

- Account for the uncountable. You might not assign economic value to every externality, but you and your management team can identify these economic values, think about them, and take them into account. The fact is even management accounting is not just about the numbers; it's about the conversations those numbers support, and the decisions the conversations enable. The key: Don't think of this as a chore. Think of it as an opportunity to see business opportunities that others might not see.

- Be transparent. Use open-book management[3] inside your company and err on the side of disclosure in external communications. Internally, this helps your people understand what's needed to innovate—in the right directions—even when you're not there to guide them. Externally—well, you can't hide anymore in the wireless world, even if you wanted to—so you might as well tell the truth.

> **...you can't hide anymore in the wireless world, even if you wanted to—so you might as well tell the truth.**

TRUTH

47

Investing in green and attracting green investment

Most people—even those who should know better—assume that "environment" is a cost, and that you have to sacrifice profit to avoid harming the environment. That thinking is a holdover from the last century (or two!) and just isn't supported by the evidence; good green efforts can produce competitive financial returns—both for your business and the economy in which it operates. Invest "green"—in resource efficient operations, for example, or low carbon-risk companies—and use your money to maximize both financial returns and environmental benefits.

How to make money and influence people—Investing in better environmental performance isn't just a good idea; it might be your fiduciary duty (see Truth 49, "Fiduciary duty"). Owners and shareholders will grow impatient, I predict, with managers who fail to capture the attractive returns and reduced risk that can result from improved environmental performance.

Your environmental performance influences who buys your product (see Truth 19, "Reaching conscious consumers") and who invests in you. Investors, both individuals and large institutional investors, increasingly favor companies and funds that reflect their values, and that look like good values in uncertain times (see Truth 50, "Certainty in the face

> Owners and shareholders will grow impatient, I predict, with managers who fail to capture the attractive returns and reduced risk....

of uncertainty"). *Socially Responsible Investment (SRI)* assets in the United States rose from $639 billion in 1995 to $2.71 trillion in 2007. From 2005 to 2007 alone, SRI assets increased more than 18 percent, whereas the broader universe of professionally managed assets increased less than 3 percent. Roughly 11 percent of assets under professional management in the U.S.—nearly one out of every nine dollars—are now involved in SRI.[1] To access this capital market, you need to show investors that you can maximize both financial and environmental returns.

"Green is green"—As GE CEO Jeff Immelt says, "green is green"—the green of environmental performance can deliver the green of bottom-line profit. Here are some ideas to consider as you try to harvest that bounty.

- Drop the assumption that environmental performance will cost you money—or even that you'll have to sacrifice near-term profits for long-term. Treat it as an investment, not a cost, and assess your opportunities as you would for any investment.

...the green of environmental performance can deliver the green of bottom-line profit.

- Learn to speak "CFO." Understand what your CFO needs to know—and how [s]he needs you to present the opportunity costs of green initiatives and the potential benefits.

- Calculate ROI, not years to payback. A three-year payback might seem like a long time, but 33 percent per year ROI—the same thing—is pretty nice pickings for legal, low-risk investments.

- Base your analyses on life-cycle costs, not first cost—even in the current survival economy.

- Compare each option to a range of other alternatives, including doing nothing.

- Capitalize the operating cost-savings of real-estate holdings. Lower energy costs means higher operating margins, which means higher property value because those are usually a multiple of operating margins.

- Present comprehensive analyses and solutions that include specific implementation steps.

- Tunnel through the cost barrier by analyzing and selecting *combinations* of measures rather than one at a time; the right measures, in the right combinations, in the right sequence, can produce significantly higher ROI than individual measures alone. "The only moderately more-efficient house and car do cost more to build, but when designed as whole systems, the super-efficient house and car can often cost less than the original, unimproved versions."[1]

- Use reality-based accounting (see Truth 46, "Reality-based accounting") to present a more complete cost-benefit analysis that at least lists and documents intangibles and risks for management's consideration, even if you can't put a financial value on them. The business case is never only financial!

- Make your company a good company to invest in. Present compelling value to all types of investors, including Socially Responsible Investment (SRI) fund investors, and to Wall Street analysts if you're a public company and owners and shareholders if you're a private company.

- Think about where you invest *your* money. Hedging your bets is all well and good, but do your investments support your strategy? And your values?

- Ask yourself these questions to see if your company passes the test:

  - Does your company contribute to solving global problems?

  - Will your company perform well in a "bright green future"?[2]

  - Will your company adapt well to an uncertain future?

Carbon trading and offsets

Carbon trading and offsets are two major strategies for managing greenhouse gas emissions. They're indirect, compared to "actual" reduction strategies, and controversial, but they're poised to become an important part of the policy mix. Carbon trading is a policy-driven mechanism to reduce carbon emissions; a governing body sets an emissions "cap," and issues or sells credits, or emissions allowances. The cap ideally decreases over time, adding pressure for emission reductions. Companies can stay within those allowances by cutting their emissions, or by buying allowances from companies that don't need them (usually because they've reduced their own emissions), or both.[1]

Carbon offsets are financial instruments that represent the GHG emission-reductions resulting from investment in projects such as energy efficiency and renewable energy, forestry projects, methane abatement, and fuel switching. Organizations and individuals purchase offsets to reduce their carbon impacts more easily—or more economically—than by actually reducing their own emissions. (But offsets are not without controversy, as discussed here.)

Money makes the world go round—Carbon is taking on economic value. The global carbon market was worth approximately US$11 billion in 2005, US$31 billion in 2006, and US$64 billion in 2007; major growth is forecast as markets move from voluntary to mandatory.[2] Carbon markets provide financial incentives to embed GHG emissions reduction into normal business decisions; mandatory carbon markets. It's not just an environmental issue anymore.

Markets and mechanisms—Know when to use trading and offsets. First measure your emissions, then reduce them as much as possible, and *then* trade your reductions or offset your remaining emissions.

There are two types of carbon markets: regulatory and voluntary. The major carbon trading markets currently are the following:

First measure your emissions, then reduce them as much as possible, and *then* trade your reductions or offset your remaining emissions.

- Regulatory
  - Kyoto Protocol's Clean Development Mechanism, regulated by the UN
  - Kyoto Protocol's Joint Implementation
  - European Union Emissions Trading Scheme (EUETS)
  - California AB32: The first mandatory U.S. emissions cap
  - The Regional Greenhouse Gas Initiative (RGGI)
  - Western Climate Initiative
- Voluntary
  - Chicago Climate Exchange, a private, contractual cap and trade system where members trade allowances with each other
  - The Climate Registry
  - Voluntary "over-the-counter" offsets

Under cap and trade schemes, a governing body distributes carbon credits through auctions and assignments. In auctions, emitters bid to purchase credits or emissions allowances; with assignments, the governing body assigns credits to emitters, often based on historical or baseline emission levels. (We favor auctions—because they more effectively harness the power of markets—and regulated markets that rapidly ratchet down the caps to drive prices and innovation.)

Cap and Dividend, another market-based approach proposed in the United States, caps fossil fuel supplies "upstream" (at the point of fossil fuel creation or import) instead of downstream at the point of combustion, and puts auction revenues in trust, to be paid out evenly to all U.S. citizens.[3]

Offsets: Modern Indulgences?—Carbon trading and offsets are controversial. George Monbiot likens offsets to 15th-century church indulgences, allowing the wealthy to buy their way out of behavior changes. "It sounds great. Without requiring any social or political change, and at a tiny cost to the consumer, the problem of climate change is solved. Having handed over a few quid, we can all sleep easy again."[4] Offsets are largely unregulated, and some firms have been caught selling offsets that offered no "additional" carbon reductions.[5] Forestry projects—a common source of offsets—can have undesirable effects, like land use changes in ecologically sensitive areas. The timing of these projects poses problems, too. Trees take time to mature, and meanwhile, additional carbon is pumped into the atmosphere, which continues to contribute to climate change.

In defense of offsets—GHG emitters can invest in offsets to drive down emissions faster than their own reduction activities would produce. Dedicated purchasers sometimes withdraw emissions trading credits from the market, hoping to drive up carbon prices up and create additional incentives for others to reduce their emissions, and "create a connection between the voluntary and regulated carbon markets."[6]

One thing about offsets is not controversial: Make sure your carbon offset projects are vetted by qualified third-party verification services.

What's the best way for your company to navigate all this controversy? First reduce your emissions (see Truth 15, "Reducing your carbon footprint"). Use offsets as a last resort.

What you need to do—When you're ready to consider carbon trading (and I suspect you will be soon):

■ Approach carbon trading as a business opportunity, not as a cost. If your performance is better than the rest of your trading market, you can sell extra emission credits to your competitors and reap multiple benefits: revenue from the trades, savings from both the energy savings that drove the reductions, and not having to purchase offsets to meet targets.

■ Ultimately, you need to decide whether to take action now or wait until you have to. The benefit of getting in the trading game early is practice and preparation for mandatory regulation. "The particulars differ," the *McKinsey Quarterly* notes, "but the bottom line is the same: emitting carbon and other substances will become more expensive, and shareholders want to know how executives plan to manage these costs."[7]

■ Build carbon trading and offsets into your planning process.

■ Engage your CFO, controller, and general manager. This is a financial issue; it's not just an environmental issue anymore.

TRUTH

Fiduciary duty

Corporate management has indispensable latitude in making everyday decisions, but some decisions go beyond management discretion to constitute negligence of material risks, and violation of fiduciary duty to shareholders. Executives and directors of corporations with fiduciary duty to company shareholders now face a new challenge: the perception that they might be violating that duty if they don't adequately prepare for such potential risks as climate change-related disruption of supply chains and stricter enforcement of environmental regulations.

Few electronics firms were ready for the European Union's Waste Electrical and Electronic Equipment (WEEE) directive. Though they knew it was coming, more than 40 percent of manufacturers were unprepared—with one-third of industry revenues on the line. As my colleagues and I argued in *The Wall Street Journal*:

> "[T]his train wreck was not only foreseeable but avoidable—and perhaps avoidable at a profit.... The electronics industry is just one example of an industry failing to keep up with increasing environmental-protection requirements.... The challenge to senior executives and boards is to steer away from the collision course with a set of global trends that many have evaluated incorrectly."[1]

Preparing for the inevitable—Just as you need balanced books, you need a clear record of responsible environmental performance. Think of it this way: If you leave money on the table by, for example, failing to invest in low-risk, high-ROI, energy-efficiency measures, shareholders might feel unhappy that you're sending potential dividends to utilities, waste haulers, or oil companies instead of into *their* pockets.

Event horizon—That's the bad news: Boards and executives are exposed when material risks are unanticipated and not prepared for. However, this is an avoidable risk; and when it comes to environmental risks, proper green fiduciary duty can create significant business opportunities, in addition to cost avoidance. Consider this, for example: If nearly half the electronics industry wasn't ready for the WEEE directive, more than half was.

Because more regulations and market challenges are coming, just clearing the hurdle in front of you isn't enough—you need to create a system for staying ahead of continually rising expectations (see Truth 32, "Clearing the rising bar").

Regulations, incentives, markets—Who is going to enforce the fiduciary duty around environmental performance? Surprise: It's not just government.

I expect that shareholder lawsuits will play an increasing role in pushing companies that don't figure this out on their own. Because shareholders often bear the consequences of company actions, they have the power—and standing—to challenge management that they believe is negligent. (Failure, error, and miscalculation are not actionable. Willful disregard of significant and avoidable hazard might well be.)

The other force to reckon with is the insurance industry. Swiss Re, the world's largest reinsurance company (which set up a unit in 2001 to look at the corporate implications of global warming), famously notified its customers that it might choose to decline Directors and Officers (D&O) insurance to companies that fail to competently address the risks of climate change. Would you think that would get some attention in boardrooms? It did.

And then there's the Carbon Beta. The investment analysts firm Innovest Strategic Value Advisors developed this ranking of companies' "carbon-related risk," expressed as a percentage of profit. The gaps are staggering; the exposure of publicly traded construction materials companies, for example, ranges from 1.2 percent to 21.3 percent of EBITDA, and for metals and mining companies, from 1.3 percent to 46.2 percent![2] If all the firms were pulling comparably high numbers, you might decline to invest in the sector; if only a few are, you might question—or challenge—the competence of their management.

Pay attention!—Some risks to watch in the near future include the following:

- **Carbon**—If you're not tracking your carbon emissions and don't at least have your footprint measured in the next few years, you are at risk because carbon caps or taxes are coming.

- **Energy security**—Whether the price of oil is up or down, whether peak oil production has happened or will happen, the fossil fuel market is volatile and is a source of global insecurity. Diversify by investing in low-carbon and renewable energy alternatives.

- **Water**—Water is the next carbon.[3] And water use is bound up with energy use (to pump, heat, cool, and treat it); though, unlike energy, living things don't have substitutes for water. What risks would disrupted water supplies present to your business?

- **Restricted materials**—The EU's RoHS directive (Restriction on Hazardous Substances) bans lead, mercury, cadmium, hexavalent chromium, brominated flame retardants (polybrominated biphenyls (PBB), and polybrominated diphenyl ethers (PBDE). How can you anticipate what might be next—and turn that to your design advantage?

- **"License to operate"**—What would happen to your business if you could no longer do business with Europe, China—or parts of the United States—due to rising regulatory hurdles that you weren't prepared to meet?

What you need to do—Here are four steps to help you face—and get ahead of—these challenges:

1. **Understand the drivers**—Surprises like the EU directives are predictable, not random. Those who understood the EU's drivers best saw WEEE/RoHS coming, aligned their design trajectory with the future regulatory trajectory, eliminated a random factor in their product development cycle, and shifted budget from lawyers and lobbyists to engineers and marketers.

2. **Drop the assumptions. Face the facts**—The notion that better environmental performance reduces financial performance is rooted in habit, not evidence. It's easy to make design improvements that cost more. It's more challenging—and more profitable—to integrate "green" into the design process, by including stakeholder expectations and sustainability requirements into design specification from the beginning.

3. **Design what works—before it's demanded**—It will happen eventually; industrial systems are more pliable than the biochemical requirements of living systems. The only question

is how quickly and how painfully? It might seem unreasonable. It might be hard. But it will come—and what if your competitors figure out how to get there first? (How many more industries will the United States have to lose before we understand this?)

4. **Steer by the logic, not the thresholds**—Environmental regulatory policy has focused on a political and scientific process of setting acceptable thresholds for problematic materials, which is always a compromise (usually a painful one) always uncertain and unsettled, and ripe for litigation. The smartest companies will "answer to a higher authority"—the physics and evolutionary biology that constitute the unrepealable laws of nature—and one that can make compelling business sense as well. Just ask DuPont's CEO and CFO about the business implications of DuPont's "unreasonable" commitment to "zero waste."

TRUTH

Certainty in the face of uncertainty

We know this, with certainty: The world in which we will spend the rest of our lives will be an uncertain and unpredictable place, perhaps more so than any time in living memory. And that's saying something! We hear about dramatic, seemingly random events all the time, and we're still surprised by them. The list of uncertainties is long and growing. Energy is an uncertainty—whether the concern is supply or price. Add to the mix: discontinuous political and technological change; rapid population and economic growth in China, India, Brazil, and elsewhere; demographic shifts that yield younger populations in the developing world and aging populations in the advanced economies; potential political instability in critical regions such as the Middle East; and of course climate change—or "global weirding," as Jay Ogilvy, Dean of Presidio Graduate School of Business, has called it—and the potential disruption of the Gulf Stream.

Actually, it's not all random and chaotic (though the media might sometimes give you that impression), and there are ways to navigate these storms. First, recognize what *is* certain, even in the midst of uncertainty. Where can you find that certainty? The best place I know is in fundamental, undisputed scientific principles in a chain of reasoning that flows from the certainty of the physics, chemistry, biology, and ecology that underlie the uncertainties of the human economy (see Truth 24, "Biomimicry—learning from life"). Regulations and markets change, but the lessons of nature's laws are inescapable—and crystal clear—even in uncertain economic times.

...learn to anticipate the "inevitable surprises" coming your way, so you can operate with some degree of perspective and choice while others are wondering what hit them.

Second, learn to anticipate the "inevitable surprises" coming your way, so you can operate with some degree of perspective and choice while others are wondering what hit them.

Preparing for the future—The foundation for certainty in the face of uncertainty is to set goals and make policies based on physical reality—in other words, rely on the things we know are certain. One of the best ways I know is to learn and apply the Natural Step (TNS) management framework, which grounds business thinking in the indisputable scientific reality of the first and second laws of thermodynamics:

1. Energy and matter are neither created nor destroyed. Only their forms can be modified.

2. Energy and matter tend to "run down," meaning that everything has a tendency to disperse.

From these principles, TNS has distilled four "system conditions"—conditions of success—for sustainable organizations and societies:

Nature must

1. Concentrations of substances extracted from the Earth's crust.

2. Concentrations of substances produced by society.

3. Degradation by physical means.

And in a sustainable society

4. People are not subject to conditions that systematically undermine their capacity to meet their needs.

(I suggest adding a fifth "system condition for sustainability"—profitability. You can be the greenest company in the world, but if you're not sustainable—in the classic business sense—you're not an example for anyone else to emulate.)

Putting TNS to work—Here's how to apply the Natural Step:

■ Because if we know that heavy mined metals (such as lead, mercury, or cadmium) mined from the Earth's crust can't be safely metabolized by living systems, will accumulate in their tissues, and that "safe thresholds" can't be determined, then prudence dictates reducing economic reliance on those materials. This is why the European Union ban on such materials in electronics products, which came as a surprise to many companies, was no surprise at all to companies that had been watching the fundamentals and preparing for this "inevitable surprise."

- Ask yourself, "What business am I really in?" What is the value that you provide to your customers, and how can you do that better, and more profitably, in the face of tumultuous change? For example, is the pulp and paper industry in the business of turning trees into paper products? Or is it in the business of managing forest ecosystems and society's fiber recycling systems? Is the automobile industry in the business of selling cars? Or is it moving people (mass transit)? Or ensuring access (urban planning)? The questions build from there, but the point is that when you identify the core purpose driving your business, you can set a course that both steers you through uncertainty and builds business value.

- Lead, don't follow. Some companies wait and react to regulation and market shifts. Some companies define the way forward by making a strategic asset out of integrating the laws of nature into their operating systems. These leaders are creating new profit centers out of unprecedented resource efficiency.

- Trim your sails, be efficient, and eliminate waste—of all kinds.

- Study companies that have led the way through uncertain times (using the Natural Step or other frameworks). Examples include Toyota, Nike, IKEA, Electrolux, Norm Thompson, Interface, ShoreBank Pacific, Scandic Hotels, General Electric, Wal-Mart, and many others (some mentioned in this book and some not).

- Take your leadership team—and eventually your entire workforce—through the TNS training, either live or online.[1]

- Diversify your strategies. Just as the diverse populations of plants and animals in natural ecosystems, each in their ecological niche, enable the system to adapt and thrive in the face of inevitable change, diverse strategies are an essential part of leadership in uncertain times.

TRUTH

51

Scenario planning

"We don't like their sound, and guitar music is on the way out." Decca Recording Co. rejecting the Beatles, 1962. "With over 50 foreign cars already on sale here, the Japanese auto industry isn't likely to carve out a big slice of the U.S. market." *BusinessWeek*, 1958.

The problem with predicting the future is that it's so easy to be wrong—leaving your business at risk and leaving money on the table. In fact, your chances of getting it right are next to zero in the face of infinite possible futures. Environmental uncertainties such as climate change, energy prices, new regulations, population growth, and shifting consumer demands make for an especially unpredictable playing field.

Scenario planning[1] is a method for identifying and evaluating potential strategies that can help you chart your course into an uncertain future. First used for military strategy, scenario planning rose to prominence when Royal Dutch/Shell used the technique to foresee the OPEC oil crisis in the early 1970s. Few oil companies had a possible embargo and shortages on their radar, and Shell reportedly weathered the storm better than others.

Scenarios are *not* predictions. Although planning teams might see elements of their scenarios come to bear, according to seasoned practitioners, it's rare to see entire scenarios unfold as envisioned. And that's not the point; scenarios are tools to expand your thinking about possible futures, diversify your contingency plans, and calibrate your senses to recognize which future you are entering. The outcomes of planning sessions help you prepare for and confront plausible though unlikely future events as well as the obvious and probable ones.

Planning for the future—Scenario planning isn't just speculation; as developed by Shell, it uses a systematic process to expand imagination and develop options. Although you might want consulting support to push you beyond your comfort zone, the approach is simple enough that you can start on your own:

1. Gather a diverse team. Scenario planning usually requires a group setting and is best done with participants of diverse age, gender, cultural background, and role within the company—or outside it.

2. Brainstorm "driving forces." What forces could significantly affect your organization? Common categories include economic, environmental, social, technological, and political influences. Consider potential drivers: How fast will certain technologies be adopted? Will specific countries become more cooperative or hostile to your interests? How will changes in wealth distribution affect your business?

3. Choose pairs of driving forces—most likely to cause significant changes surrounding your business, and distinctly different or even seemingly unrelated from each other—to define your initial scenarios. Use the two forces to create a two-by-two matrix that displays one possible scenario in each quadrant. The scenarios don't need to be probable, just plausible; stretch boundaries here.

4. Flesh out each scenario by creating a richly textured narrative. For example, what might fashion trends or political moods be like in each scenario? How might consumer behavior be affected? Restrain judgment and give imagination free reign. Communicate your scenarios creatively to other stakeholders; images, narrative writing, or even skits can work well.

5. Do it again—using one or two more pairs of drivers as axes for additional sets of possible scenarios.

6. Allow generous time for people to think them through after a group discussion—even using a two-day process to allow participants to "sleep on it."

Put your scenarios to work—How do you use your four (or more) possible scenarios? First, you can use them to help evaluate your business strategies. Let's say your company sources an important raw material from overseas. In which scenarios does that strategy work well, and in which are you vulnerable? What would you have to adjust for it to be a more robust business strategy? Which strategies have the best shot at viability in multiple possible futures?

Next, they can provide early warnings that the world is moving in the direction of your scenarios. Specifically, you can identify indicators that tell you which direction you're moving toward. For example, you might observe how rapidly new technology innovation is accelerating or decelerating. Is regulation increasing or decreasing? Can you see patterns in seemingly "random" events?

Be flexible. Scenario planning can support scenario-based thinking where you and your team constantly evaluate and adjust business strategies on-the-fly. There will still be surprises, but scenario thinking can help you adapt quickly and hopefully more profitably (see Truth 52, "Future proofing").

How does scenario planning affect profit? As a high-level strategy tool, it is hard to quantify the value of scenario planning; the benefits are often anecdotal. For example, people still argue over how much the Royal Dutch/Shell scenarios actually affected profits during the OPEC crisis. But it's a good bet that forewarned is forearmed.

> ...it's a good bet that forewarned is forearmed.

How can scenario practitioners make sure their audiences interpret their scenarios as intended? You can't, but just create scenarios and hand off a report to executives to figure out what to do with your "prediction." Prepare them so they understand what they're getting, and how to use it. Even better, include them in the development of the scenarios from the beginning.

Next steps

- Read some examples of scenario-planning projects—like the role scenario planning played in South Africa in the peaceful transition from apartheid to a multiracial government.[2]

- Practice an example on your own. Team efforts typically make the best scenarios, but you'll get a feel for the process.

- Study *The Art of the Long View*, the definitive "how to" guide from scenario planning veteran Peter Schwartz at Global Business Network.[3]

- Check out Jamais Cascio's application of scenario planning to Green Tomorrows: http://openthefuture. com/2007/11/green_tomorrows_the_scenarios.html.

TRUTH

52

Future proofing

Here's the bad news: After you acknowledge nature's certainties and uncertainties, and use scenario planning to help you imagine the array of possible futures, you need to create strategies that will work, no matter what the future holds. Here's the good news: Although you can't anticipate everything, you can build a resilient company that responds quickly and profitably to "inevitable surprises."

If you can find ways to anticipate and prepare, you can insulate yourself from uncertainties that will bedevil others. For example, if your company phases toxins out of your products—and does it efficiently, economically, and in support of your brand—you'll be in good shape whether future regulations outlaw them.

The term "future-proofing" was coined, as far as I can tell, by software designers to describe code that would continue to function well, and be easy to adapt, in the face of ever-changing tools, protocols, expectations, and risks.

With this definition as a benchmark, future proofing is extremely important for businesses facing the ever-changing challenges of "green" that I discuss throughout this book.

Reducing risk—Future proofing your business is your key to reducing risk, building strategies, and operating in ways that hold the greatest chance of viability in the face of futures that—I guarantee it—will surprise you!

And the key to future proofing is to build your business on a firm foundation that is not subject to the whims of either fashion or politics (see Truth 50, "Certainty in the face of uncertainty") and to pursue strategies that carry good odds of success in multiple possible futures.

> ...the key to future proofing is to build your business on a firm foundation that is not subject to the whims of either fashion or politics....

For me, the best bet is the playbook hiding in plain sight: the nearly four billion years of trial, error, learning, and refinement conducted by Earth's living systems. Why reinvent the wheel (as I asked in Truth 9, "Secrets hiding in plain sight") when the R&D has already been done?

Bringing it home—That's the big picture. Here's your local challenge:

Figure out what aspects of your business must be unchangeable bedrock—the non-negotiable principles, core values, and core value propositions on which your very identity depends—and which ones are adaptable (or expendable). Whole industries have suffered or even died for getting this wrong (railroads that didn't realize they were in the transportation business, not the train business,[1] for example). On the other hand, companies have thrived by getting it right; Nordstrom wouldn't be Nordstrom if it ditched its core strategy of providing exceptional customer service.

So, what makes you you? Or, as I often ask our clients, "What are you really here to do?" Your job is to hold fiercely to core values and core identity, and to be ready to adapt or abandon the aspects that are not part of your core—both specific business practices and peripheral products and services—while continuing to deliver and build value in changing markets, and a changing world.

It's the law—Similarly, your job is to operate your business in harmony with the law—the laws of nature.

When your company is not in tune with the laws of nature (for example, if it depends on toxic materials, uses lots of nonrenewable resources, or still creates "waste"), you're at risk with regulators, competitors, customers, and simply the resources you need to operate. Operate in tune with the laws of nature, and the risks diminish. You'll be well ahead of changing regulatory expectations, while your competitors are stuck playing catch-up.

As industry moves toward sustainability in a carbon-constrained world, you need to be ready to adapt to changes in carbon regulation and natural resources. To do that, you need strategies that work in multiple scenarios (see Truth 51, "Scenario planning"), because you'll never know which future will unfold—and you need to be ready to continually rethink and adapt those strategies further.

What you need to do—How can you future-proof your organization? Well, you can't with absolute certainty, but here are some steps that can improve your odds:

- Be "lean and green." Create systems that allow your company to be smart and agile enough to integrate unexpected changes. Change *will* happen no matter how prepared you are.

- Ground your business in physical reality, not just economic reality (see Truth 50).

- Engage everyone in trend-watching. It's not just a job for the executive suite. Employees who know and share your mission, and who understand—and helped build—your strategic framework, will spot issues that you might not see. Your company is only as smart and agile as the people who support it (see Truth 41, "Engaging stakeholders").

- Build contingency plans for unexpected changes—for stock market investors, ecosystems, and business people. But even though you're armed with diverse strategies, don't assume that you've covered all your bases. Refresh those plans regularly, and never stop thinking about new strategies as the changes roll in!

> Your company is only as smart and agile as the people who support it.

- Measure the right things! (see Truth 42, "Keeping score").

- Be great, not run of the mill. Create "Big, Hairy, Audacious Goals" (BHAG)[2] and share them with the world. No matter what future unfolds, keep core values and goals intact.

Nature bats last—You can be sure of this: The laws of nature will apply no matter how the future unfolds. As my wife reminds me: "You can't break the laws of nature; you can only break yourself against them."

Appendix A

References

Truth 1

1. General Electric Ecomagination, http://ge.ecomagination.com/site/ #vision/revenue.

2. Wal-Mart Unveils *Packaging Scorecard to Suppliers*, 2006, http://walmartstores.com/FactsNews/NewsRoom/6039.aspx.

3. General Electric, "Increase revenues from ecoimagination products," http://ge.ecomagination.com/site/#vision/revenue.

Truth 2

1. Natural Marketing Institute, *Understanding the LOHAS Market*, www.lohas.com/about.html.

2. Cleantech Group, January 2009, http://cleantech.com/about/ pressreleases/ 010609.cfm.

Truth 3

1. Charles M. Schwab, *The Best Place to Succeed Is Where You Are with What You Have*, quoted by Burton Folsom in *Entrepreneurs Vs. the State* (Young America's Foundation, October 1989).

Truth 5

1. U.S. Environmental Protection Agency, *Climate Change: Basic Information*, www.epa.gov/climatechange/basicinfo.html, April 2008.

2. Climate Change 2007 Synthesis Report, Contribution of Working Groups I, II, and III to the 4th Assessment Report of the Intergovernmental Panel on Climate Change (IPCC), www.ipcc.ch/ipccreports/ar4-syr.htm.

3. Deborah Zabarenko, *Could Arctic Ice Melt Spawn New Kind of Cold War?*, Reuters, www.reuters.com/article/environmentNews/ idUSN0731901820080309.

4. IPCC, ibid.

Truth 6

1. *Buckminster Fuller and the Game of the World*, by Medard Gabel, in *Buckminster Fuller: Anthology for the New Millennium*, edited by Thomas Zung, St. Martin's Press, NY, 2001.

Truth 7

1. The Natural Step, www.naturalstep.org.

2. BHAG (pronounced bee-hag, shorthand for "Big, Hairy, Audacious Goal") is a 10- to 30-year objective—such as a big mountain to climb—that serves as a unifying focal point of effort, galvanizing people, and creating team spirit. It is crisp, compelling, and easy to understand. www.jimcollins.com/lab/buildingVision/p2.html.

3. James C. Collins and Jerry I. Porras, *Built to Last: Successful Habits of Visionary Companies.*

4. A Declaration of Leadership, www.declarationofleadership.com.

Truth 8

1. WEEE (Waste Electronics and Electrical Equipment Directive), RoHS (Restriction on Hazardous Substances), and REACH (Registration, Evaluation, Authorization, and Restriction of Chemicals) are forward-looking European Union directives that have had global impact as they've rippled through electronics, chemical, and other industry's supply chains.

Truth 9

1. Gerry Mooney, www.mooneyart.com/gravity/historyof_01.html, 1986.

2. The Four System Conditions, www.thenaturalstep.org//the-system-conditions.

Truth 10

1. IKEA Social and Environmental Responsiblity Brochure (2004), http://www.ikea-group.ikea.com/repository/documents/922.pdf

2. *Cleaner Production and Eco-Efficiency,* by WBCSD and UNEP Industry and Environment Program, www.wbcsd.org/includes/getTarget. asp?type=d&id=ODcxMg, September 1998.

Truth 11

1. RU Ayres, National Academy of Engineering.

2. For more detail, check out *Waste: What Is It Really Costing You?,* www.epa.state.oh.us/opp/planning/fact72.pdf.

3. Friend, Gil. CST XI.

4. ibid, Manos, Anthony.

5. Design for Environment is a process for incorporating environmental considerations into products and services before they enter the production phase. It typically includes design for environmental manufacturing (including design for disassembly), design for environmental packaging, and design for disposal and recyclability. See Kenneth Crow, www.npd-solutions.com/dfe.html, and Truths 24-28.

6. "Five Great Wastes," *Chauncey Bell Blog: Exploring Social, Commerical, and Technological Innovation,* http://chaunceybell.wordpress.com/2007/08/22/five-great-wastes/.

Truth 12

1. U.S. Environmental Protection Agency WaterSense, www.epa.gov/WaterSense/pp/index.htm.

Truth 13

1. Toyota, www.toyota.co.jp/en/vision/production_system/.

2. www.swmas.co.uk/Lean_Tools/The_7_Wastes.php.

3. http://chaunceybell.wordpress.com/2007/08/22/five-great-wastes/.

Truth 19

1. LOHAS Online, *LOHAS Background*, www.lohas.com, 2008.

2. Kaoru Kunita, *LOHAS Takes Japan*, 2008.

Truth 20

1. LCA is an analytical technique used to assess the environmental impacts associated with a product, process, or service, by compiling an inventory of relevant energy and material inputs and environmental releases at each stage of a product's life cycle, from cradle to grave. LCA evaluates the potential environmental impacts associated with identified inputs and releases, and interpreting the results to guide design decisions. http://www.epa.gov/nrmrl/lcaccess/.

2. Gil Friend, *From Life Cycle Assessment to Life Cycle Thinking*, New Bottom Line Volume 5.3, January 30, 1996.

3. William McDonough and Michael Braungart, *The Anatomy of Transformation*, 2002, www.mcdonough.com/writings/anatomy_transformation.htm.

4. The Natural Step "system conditions" provide a powerful guide: http://www.thenaturalstep.org/our-approach#next-steps.

Truth 21

1. *HP Innovates "Closed Loop" Inkjet Cartridge Recycling Program, Gives Plastic Water Bottles Second Life*, www.hp.com/hpinfo/newsroom/press/2008/ 080130xa.html.

2. Patagonia Common Threads Garment Recycling Program, www.patagonia.com/web/us/patagonia.go?assetid=1956.

3. The states of California, Maine, Maryland, and Washington, and New York City, were among the first to introduce e-waste policies. Policies vary in structure and form. www.e-takeback.org/docs%20open/Toolkit_Legislators/state%20legislation/state_leg_main.htm.

Truth 22

1. *Popular Mechanics Breakthrough Awards-Thinking Big*, 2007, www.popularmechanics.co.za/content/general/singlepage.asp?fid=1275&pno=1.

2. Business.gov, Servicizing, www.business.gov/guides/environment/product-development/servicizing.html.

3. Esty and Winston, *Green to Gold*, 2006.

Truth 23

1. Treehugger, "Hertz Rolls Out Car-Sharing Program to Compete with Zipcar," (2009), http://www.treehugger.com/files/2009/01/hertz-car-sharing.php.

Truth 24

1. Mercedes Bionic Concept Car, Car Buyer's Notebook, http://tinyurl.com/5l9gvm, 2005.

2. Janine Benyus, *Biomimicry: Innovation Inspired by Nature*, Harper Perennial, 2002.

3. Jer Faludi, *Biomimicry for Green Design (A How-To)*, 2005. www.worldchanging.com/archives/003680.html.

4. Thomas E. Graedel and Braden R. Allenby, *Industrial Ecology*, Second Edition, Prentice-Hall, 2002.

5. *What Do You Mean by the Term Biomimicry? A Conversation with Janine Benyus*. Biomimicry Institute. www.tinyurl.com/9gqatg.

6. *Olympic Swimsuit Mimics Shark Skin*, Natural History Museum, August 15, 2008, www.nhm.ac.uk/about-us/news/2008/august/olympic-swimsuit-mimics-shark-skin.html.

7. *Nature's 100 Best*, Gunter Pauli et al, http://n100best.org.

Truth 25

1. Jamais Cascio, *Open the Future: The Cheeseburger Footprint*, http://openthefuture.com/cheeseburger_CF.html.

2. Global Footprint Network, Glossary, updated 2009, www.footprintnetwork.org/gfn_sub.php?content=glossary.

3. Global Footprint Network, *The Ecological Footprint Atlas*, 2008, www.footprintnetwork.org/download.php?id=506.

4. Global Footprint Network, *Humanity's Growing Demand on Nature Approaching Critical Threshold*, 2008, www.footprintnetwork.org/en/index.php/GFN/press/humanitys_growing_demand_on_nature_approaching_critical_threshold_report_fi.

5. *The Wall Street Journal, Six Products, Six Carbon Footprints*, October 2008.

6. Gil Friend and William Reed, *Embodied Energy Architectural Design*, Volume 72, Issue 3 (2002).

7. The meager energy yield of corn-to-ethanol is one of several arguments (along with concern over diversion of food to fuel) against over-reliance on that fuel source.

8. Global Footprint Network Application Standards, www.footprintnetwork.org/gfn_sub.php?content=standards.

Truth 26

1. McDonough Braungart, *Design Chemistry, Glossary of Key Terms*. (The term was coined by Walter R. Stahel in 1970 and popularized by William McDonough and Michael Braungart in their 2002 book, *Cradle to Cradle: Remaking the Way We Make Things*. See also www.mbdc.com/c2c_home.htm.)

2. Zeftron Nylon is used in carpeting. At the end of the carpet's life, the plastics can be broken down into original polymers and remade into new nylon. www.zeftronnylon.com.

3. McDonough Braungart, *Design Chemistry, Glossary of Key Terms*.

4. The practice of recycling a material in such a way that much of its inherent value is lost. McDonough Braungart, *Design Chemistry, Glossary of Key Terms*.

5. *Cradle to Cradle Material Flows*, www.greenblue.org/cradle_flows. html.

6. Cradle-to-Cradle certification, www.c2ccertified.com.

Truth 27

1. Ian McHarg, *Design with Nature*, Doubleday/Natural History Press 1969, Wiley 1995.

2. *Nature's Services: Societal Dependence on Natural Ecosystems*, Gretchen Daily, editor, Island Press, 1997.

Truth 28

1. Thomas Friedman, *Hot, Flat, and Crowded*, www.nytimes.com/2008/09/10/books/chapters/chapter-hot-flat-crowded.html.

2. Edward DeBono, *Lateral Thinking*, Harper Colophon, 1973.

Truth 29

1. U.S. EPA, *Environmentally Preferable Purchasing*, www.epa.gov/epp/tools/index.htm.

2. Executive Order 13423, *Strengthening Federal Environmental, Energy, and Transportation Management*, www.ofee.gov/eo/EO_13423.pdf.

3. *The Selected Works of Arne Naess*, Volumes 1-1, Springer (2005).

Truth 30

1. Eric Olson and Gil Friend, *Beyond EHS: Creating Value Through Strategic Supply Chain Partnerships*, Natural Logic, 2003.

2. Electronic Industry Citizenship Coalition: *Unified for Social Responsibility and Shared Efficiencies in the Global Electronics Supply Chain*, www.eicc.info/index.html.

3. *StopWaste Partnership Case Study: NUMMI*, www.stopwaste.org/docs/nummi.pdf.

4. *Wal-Mart Sustainable Value Networks*, walmartstores.com/Sustainability/7672.aspx.

Truth 31

1. *Wal-Mart Unveils "Packaging Scorecard" to Suppliers,* http://walmartstores.com/FactsNews/NewsRoom/6039.aspx.

2. *Wal-Mart Packaging Scorecard Changes, Progress,* November 2008, www.packworld.com/webonly-26528.

3. Lisa Everitt, *Whole Foods and Wal-Mart Execs Agree: We're Not Green,* Bnet Industries. http://industry.bnet.com/retail/1000106/ whole-foods-re-wal-mart-theyre-not-green-but-were-not-either.

4. The Natural Step, J.M. Bygg, *Construction, Sweden: A Natural Step Network Case Study,* www.thenaturalstep.org/en/usa/ jm-bygg-construction-sweden.

Truth 32

1. A wonderful phrase attributed, apparently apocryphally, to hockey great Wayne Gretsky.

Truth 33

1. *Green Dallas,* www.greendallas.net/green_standard.html.

Truth 34

1. Robin Suttell, *The True Costs of Building Green,* 2006. www.buildings. com/articles/detail.aspx?contentID=3029.

2. *Why Build Green?* Rocky Mountain Institute White Paper, www.rmi. org/images/PDFs/BuildingsLand/D02-14_WhyBuildGreen.pdf.

Truth 35

1. Rocky Mountain Institute, *Greening the Building and the Bottom Line,* 1998.

2. U.S. EPA, *Report to Congress on Indoor Air Quality. Volume II: Assessment and Control of Indoor Air Pollution,* 1989.

3. Heerwagen, J.H., *Green Buildings, Organizational Success, and Occupant Productivity,* 2000.

4. Greg Kats, *Capital E, The Costs and Financial Benefits of Green Buildings,* October 2003.

5. UC Berkeley Center for the Built Environment, *Operable Windows and Thermal Comfort,* 2006.

6. GreenSeal, www.greenseal.org/findaproduct/index.cfm.

Truth 36

1. U.S. Department of Energy, *Integrated Building Design,* May 2001.

2. Bill Reed, *Shifting Our Mental Model—Sustainability to Regeneration,* Building Research and Information, 2006, www.integrativedesign. net/files/u1/ShiftingOurMentalModel.pdf.

Truth 37

1. *Facts and Figures on E Waste and Recycling*, Electronics Take-Back Coalition, 2009. http://tinyurl.com/cz6598.

2. Singer, Michael, *Fujitsu Siemens Goes Green in Germany*, http://news.cnet.com/Fujitsu-Siemens-goes-green-in-Germany/2100-1006_3-5844181.html.

3. EnergyStar, *General Technical Overview of Power Management*, www.energystar.gov/index.cfm?c=power_mgt.pr_power_management.

4. Sun Microsystems Recognized by U.S. EPA for Surpassing Aggressive Greenhouse Gas Emissions Goal, 2008, www.sun.com/aboutsun/pr/2008-10/sunflash.20081008.1.xml.

Truth 38

1. Jason Mick, *Inside Google's Green Data Centers*, Inside Tech, October 2008.

2. Dave Ohara, *Build a Green Data Center*, Microsoft TechNet Magazine, 2007.

3. Robert L. Mitchell, *The Grill: Rocky Mountain Institute's Amory B. Lovins on the Hot Seat*, Computerworld, May 2007.

4. Steve Greenberg et al., Lawrence Berkeley National Laboratory. *Best Practices for Data Centers: Lessons Learned from Benchmarking 22 Data Centers*, 2006.

5. Data Center Power, 42U. www.42u.com/power/data-center-power.htm.

6. Robert L. Mitchell, *Seven Steps to a Green Data Center*, Computerworld, April 2007.

7. Mark Fontecchio, *Sun's Data Center Consolidation Reduces Space, Servers*, Computerworld, August 2007.

8. Robert L. Mitchell, *Power Trip: The Case for Cogeneration*, Computerworld, August 2007.

Truth 39

1. Robert L. Mitchell, Computerworld, *The Grill: Rocky Mountain Institute's Amory B. Lovins on the Hot Seat*, May 2007. (www.computerworld.com/action/article.do?command=viewArticleBasic&articleId=290732).

2. Ann Bednarz, Computerworld, *Sun's 'Open Work' Program Sheds Light on Telecommute Savings*, June 2008.

3. *Dashboards That Make a Difference*, www.businessmetabolics.com.

Truth 40

1. Katharine Esty and Mindy Gewirtz, *Creating a Culture of Employee Engagement*, June 2008, www.boston.com/jobs/nehra/062308.shtml.

2. Ibid.

3. 3M, Employee Engagement Web site, 2009, http://tinyurl.com/dezuwv.

Truth 41

1. Freeman, R. Edward, *Strategic Management: A Stakeholder Approach*, 1984.

2. Hewlett-Packard Stakeholder Advisory Council, www.hp.com/hpinfo/globalcitizenship/gcreport/globalcitizen/stakeholder/advisory.html.

Truth 42

1. Natural Logic's web-based Business Metabolics™ was built to provide just that capability. www.BusinessMetabolics.com.

Truth 43

1. JM Juran, *The Quality Control Handbook*, Fourth Edition, McGraw-Hill, 1988.

2. J. Hanhart, Ecofeedback, *Feedback as a Tool in Restoring Environmental and Humanitarian Equilibrium*, Publiek Ontwerp, 1989.

Truth 44

1. U.S. EPA's EMS Guide, www.epa.gov/ems.

2. International Organization for Standardization, www.iso.org/iso/management_standards.htm.

Truth 45

1. In 1984, a Union Carbide pesticide plant in Bhopal, India, released toxic gases into the air, exposing more than 500,000 people in one of the worst industrial disasters.

Truth 46

1. Robert F. Kennedy Jr., Commonwealth Club speech, 2002, www.commonwealthclub.org/archive/02/02-02kennedy-speech.html.

2. *STMicroelectronics Wins U.S. EPA Climate Protection Award*, 1999, www.st.com/stonline/press/news/year1999/c576h.htm.

3. Jack Stack and Bo Burlingham, *A Stake in the Outcome: Building a Culture of Ownership for the Long-Term Success of Your Business*, Broadway Business, 2003.

Truth 47

1. *Socially Responsible Investment Trends Report*, Social Investment Forum, 2007.

2. Chapter 6, *Tunneling Through the Cost Barrier*, in Amory Lovins, Hunter Lovins, Paul Hawken, *Natural Capitalism*; www.natcap.org/sitepages/pid61.php, and NBL 5.12.

Truth 48

1. British Airways Web site: http://tinyurl.com/c5n4vv (offsets) and http://tinyurl.com/cqrmqp (trading).

2. Ecosystem Marketplace and New Carbon Finance, *Forging a Frontier: State of the Voluntary Carbon Markets in 2008*, May 2008.

3. Adam Stein, Terrapass, *Latest Flavor of Carbon Legislation: Cap and Dividend*, January 2008, www.capanddividend.org.

4. George Monbiot, *Selling Indulgences*, 2006, www.monbiot.com/archives/2006/10/19/selling-indulgences.

5. "Additionality" means that an offset project is a new carbon reduction, not something that was going to "happen anyway." Some offset providers have been scrutinized for emissions reduction projects that were likely to be built anyway.

6. http://en.wikipedia.org/wiki/Carbon_offset.

7. Christoph Grobbel et al., *Preparing for a Low-Carbon Future*, McKinsey Quarterly, November 2004.

Truth 49

1. Gil Friend, Pamela Gordon, and Michael Kirschner, *Wishing Won't Make It So*, WSJ Online, August 17, 2005, http://online.wsj.com/article/SB112422524025914755.html.

2. *Carbon Beta and Equity Performance: Understanding Climate Risks & Opportunities*, Innovest Strategic Value Advisors, March 2009.

3. For more information about water risks and strategies, read Lester Brown's *Plan B 3.0: Mobilizing to Save Civilization*, New York: W.W. Norton & Company, 2008.

Truth 50

1. The Natural Step, www.naturalstep.org.

Truth 51

1. Lawrence Wilkinson, *How to Build Scenarios*, www.wired.com/wired/scenarios/build.html.

2. Adam Kahane, *Changing the Winds*, http://wholeearth.com/issue/2096/article/71/changing.the.winds.

3. Peter Schwartz and Jay Ogilvy, *Planning Your Scenarios*, www.gbn.com/consulting/article_details.php?id=24&breadcrumb=ideas.

Truth 52

1. Theodore Levitt, *Marketing Myopia*, Harvard Business Review, Sept.-Oct. 1975, www.amazon.com/Marketing-Myopia/dp/B00005REKB.

2. BHAG (pronounced bee-hag, shorthand for "Big, Hairy, Audacious Goal") is a 10- to 30-year objective—such as a big mountain to climb—that serves as a unifying focal point of effort, galvanizing people, and creating team spirit. It is crisp, compelling, and easy to understand. www.jimcollins.com/lab/buildingVision/p2.html.

A

Acknowledgments

My acknowledgments begin in the only place they can: with Nick Kordesch and Benjamin Privitt of Natural Logic, whose research, writing, editing, and thinking skills—and deep commitment to this work—made this book possible. Thanks to my editors, Rick Kughen and Beatrice Aranow, who guided me with both wisdom and grace.

I'm grateful, too, to the other staff and former staff of Natural Logic, our associates network past and present, and our board, whose experience and ideas have fed mine.

Because sustainability consulting is a field that is blessedly at least as collegial as it is competitive, I'm thankful for all I've learned and chewed on with friends, colleagues, and clients—committed, challenging, rewarding clients—too numerous to name.

I've been blessed with wise mentors, all of whose names for some reason seem to start with Bs: Gregory Bateson, Chauncey Bell, Stafford Beer, and Bucky Fuller. And one more B: Jane Byrd, my wife, thinking partner, and muse. I'm grateful for them all.

About the Author

Gil Friend is founder, President, and CEO of Natural Logic, Inc. Natural Logic provides advisory services in strategy, implementation, and performance measurement that help companies and communities prosper by embedding the laws of nature at the hearts of enterprise.

A systems ecologist and business strategist with nearly 40 years experience in business, communications, and environmental innovation, Friend combines broad business experience with unique content experience spanning strategy, systems ecology, economic development, management cybernetics, and public policy. *Tomorrow* magazine called him "One of the country's leading environmental management consultants—a real expert who combines theoretical sophistication with hands-on, in-the-trenches know-how." He is a founding board member of the Sustainable Business Alliance, Sustainable Berkeley, and the California Sustainable Business Council and serves on the executive board of OpenEco.org and the advisory boards of CleanFish, WattBot, Green World Campaign, and (past) San Francisco Mayor Gavin Newsom's Clean Tech Advisory Council. Friend served in the California Governor's Office, developing early sustainability policies and programs, was a founding board member of Internet pioneer Institute for Global Communications, was founder and Executive Director of Foundation for the Arts of Peace, and was cofounder and codirector of the Institute for Local Self-Reliance, a leading urban ecology and economic development "think-and-do tank," where he pioneered the current "green roof" trend more than 35 years ago.

Friend lectures widely on business strategy and sustainability policy and writes "The New Bottom Line" (www.natlogic.com/new-bottom-line) offering strategic perspectives on business and environment. He has contributed chapters to several books, including *Worldchanging: A User's Guide to the 21st Century, Sustainable Enterprise Report, Sustainable Enterprise Fieldbook, Sustainable Food Systems*, and *Stepping Stones*, and is the author of the forthcoming book *Profit on Purpose: Risk, Fiduciary Duty and the Laws of Nature*.

He holds an M.S. degree in systems ecology from Antioch University, has a black belt in Aikido, and is a seasoned practitioner of "The Natural Step" environmental management system.

About the Contributors

Nicholas Kordesch is a sustainability analyst at Natural Logic, where he applies his experience in environmental science, industrial ecology, business strategy, and corporate social responsibility to a wide range of clients and services. Kordesch's previous work experience includes research at UC Berkeley's Forest Pathology and Mycology Laboratory, an internship in Applied Materials' Environmental Solutions division, and content writing at the greenweb startup Greeniacs.com.

Kordesch received his master's degree from the Donald Bren School of Environmental Science and Management at UC Santa Barbara, where he focused his studies on corporate environmental management and completed a master's thesis on scenario planning for Volvo Cars' Monitoring and Concept Center. Kordesch also holds a B.S. degree in environmental sciences from UC Berkeley.

Benjamin Privitt is operations manager at Natural Logic and brings "hybrid vigor" to the team, streamlining internal processes and shepherding operations development for the company.

He previously worked as multimedia project manager, office coordinator, copywriter, and program producer at GraceCom Media broadcast production company, where he was integral to GraceCom's communication and content production, and as a production manager at Mal Warwick Associates, a certified green business that creates direct mail fundraising campaigns for nonprofit organizations.

Privitt is an MBA candidate at Bainbridge Graduate Institute, studying sustainable business with a focus on food systems and agriculture.